praise for *forgive us*

Forgive Us strikes m[...] 2008 ✓ W9-AVI-531

for—that a new gen[...]

into its calling. Seco[...]

would humble themselves, at any time and in any condition, and pray and seek God's face and turn from our wicked ways, then God will hear from heaven and will forgive us and heal our land. This book offers the church the chance to do that deep and cleansing work of repentance, not just to say we're sorry, but to truly turn from our sinful ways in true humility. The thought that God can use a repentant people in the great enterprise of repairing and redeeming the world...this should humble us. We all need this book. This is the way and we should all walk in it.

Dr. John M. Perkins, Founder, John and Vera Mae Perkins Foundation, Cofounder, Christian Community Development Association

There are sins we commit as individuals, for which we usually experience some kind of guilt. This book, on the other hand, is about sins that we, as Americans, are committing collectively and for which we as a complicit people should repent. For all of us who need to be sensitized to corporate sins and to the oppression that is perpetrated because of the evils that are inherent in many of the ways our political and economic systems function, this book is both a revelation and a call to action.

Tony Campolo, Professor of Sociology, Eastern University

Forgive Us points us to vital issues in the American evangelical world where the ball has been dropped and where various traditions may not have provided helpful direction. We are invited by the authors to repent and lament in ways that direct us to strategic opportunities to bring our Bibles and our respective doctrinal standards to the questions of yesterday, today, and tomorrow so that God's will may be done on earth as it is in heaven. These are some of the most important issues facing the church today.

Anthony B. Bradley, Associate Professor of Theology and Ethics, The King's College and author of *The Political Economy of Liberation*

There is now a great deal of talk about "the crisis in the church." Most of that talk is frivolous and too easy, propelled by manufactured solutions, business models, or cheap grace. Not here! These writers walk honestly into the failures of the church that has too long, too often, colluded with convenient exclusionary practices. This book is a recognition that serious forgiveness by God follows serious repentance. This is well-informed, highly disciplined theology applied to the lived realities of the church.

Walter Brueggemann, Columbia Theological Seminary

Forgive Us is a strikingly candid and humble admission of the where the contemporary church has been in the wrong. A remarkable quartet of authors and thought-leaders, Cannon, Harper, Jackson, and Rah use biblical examples of honest prayers to seek reconciliation and ask God to "heal our land." If you long to see the church be more than "right," but also have a right relationship with the world around us, than *Forgive Us* is a must-read!

Dave Ferguson, author of *Finding Your Way Back to God*,
lead pastor, Community Christian Church;
Spiritual Entrepreneur, NewThing

The progress from "now we see ourselves in a mirror dimly, but then face to face" does not always bring great joy. This book showed me more of myself, of my group, of my heart than I wanted to see clearly. Yet in facing and confessing the ways I have participated in other's degradation elevates us both. To ask forgiveness is to not to give up a sense of right and wrong; it is to give up a sense of arrogance and scapegoat theology. This book helps me love my neighbor better and accept God's judgment of us all.

Dr. Joel C. Hunter, Senior Pastor,
Northland — A Church Distributed

It's a daunting task, to seek to bring Christians to repentance. With great grace, the authors of *Forgive Us* reveal ways we in the US church treat as less-than-fully-human people made in the image of God. Read with an open, humble heart. And be blessed to find that lament and confession lead to healing, reconciliation, life.

Deborah Brunt, keytruths.com, author of *We Confess!*
The Civil War, the South, and the Church

At a time when evangelicals are understandably often seen as pompously pious, *Forgive Us* reads like a confessional booth. Instead of being asked to divulge their sins to us, people who don't share our Christian faith hear us admit how far too many of our predecessors and peers have grievously sinned against others and pledge to live out our faith in ways that are more tangibly aligned with the mercy and grace of Christ. This exceptional book has the power to disarm a cynical world because it is a stunning example of evangelical Christians humbly stripping off our garments of triumphalism and privilege and covering our nakedness with the sackcloth and ashes of true lament and confession.

Ken Fong, Senior Pastor, Evergreen Baptist Church of LA (Rosemead) and Executive Director, Fuller Theological Seminary's Asian American Initiative

In this book a very promising evangelical future is embodied: humble, honest, repentant, post-WASP, post-patriarchal. Evangelical sins are skewered; American (and Christian) history is recounted in terrifyingly unsentimental terms. The contrast between this kind of evangelicalism and that of the reactionary right is staggering. A must-read book.

Dr. David P. Gushee, Distinguished University Professor of Christian Ethics Director, Center for Theology and Public Life Mercer University

Forgive Us is a truly courageous and prophetic book. It calls on evangelical to go beyond paying lip service to social justice to engage collective confession for the church's complicity in racial, gender, and other forms of oppression. Through its engaged historical and social analysis, *Forgive Us* makes clear that the church must engage in deep introspection to effectively proclaim God's word. This book will challenge many because it offers no cheap grace and pulls no punches in telling the truth about the church's histories of injustice. And yet this book offers hope that through serious and engaged collective confession, Christians can finally become the people we are called to be — proclaiming God's justice throughout the world.

Andrea Smith, Board Member of North American Institute for Indigenous Theological Study and author of *Conquest: Sexual Violence and American Indian Genocide*

Forgive Us is timely and unique. It is the heart-cry of a group of friends—all scholars and justice workers in their own rights—to bring the biblical imperative of lament, confession, and repentance to key areas of American church history that are often discussed but rarely from this perspective and with such honesty and humility. It aptly calls out the savior attitude of an American church that continues to try to fix problems without recognizing its own complicated role in creating them. *Forgive Us* is a counter-narrative of confession and truth-telling that will leave you wondering why you've never heard the fuller story of so many injustices or realized how Christians have and continue to be complicit in them. It will equip and encourage you toward biblical reconciliation and peace-making as well as honest self-examination and engagement. *Forgive Us* is a much needed addition to the conversation on American religion and politics.

**Ken Wytsma is the founder of the Justice Conference
and the author of *Pursuing Justice: The Call to Live
and Die for Bigger Things***

Two women and two men, two people of color and two whites—all four US Christians—issue a powerful call for lament, forgiveness, repentance, and action for sins of injustice committed throughout the history of the United States. Surprisingly, their confession of sin is directed toward, and on behalf of, the church in the United States. They believe the integrity, and even the survival, of the US church is at stake. *Forgive Us* is a must-read for Christians in the United States.

**Curtiss Paul DeYoung, author, professor, pastor, and activist,
focused on issues of reconciliation and social justice, currently
serving at the Community Renewal Society in Chicago**

Forgive Us is courageous, honest, painful, and absolutely essential. Courageous because the authors know there will be pushback from some parts of the Body; honest and painful because it tells hardball truths about the sins of the church; and absolutely essential because it calls the church to do what must be done in the face of great sin: lament, confess, and repent. Perhaps on the other side, forgiveness awaits us, as well as another opportunity to tell good news—the good news of Jesus.

**Al Tizon, Ronald J. Sider Associate, Professor of Holistic
Ministry, Palmer Theological Seminary of Eastern University**

A powerful urgent plea for Christians to repent. Biblical faith demands that we listen carefully and respond positively.

Ronald J. Sider, Senior Distinguished Professor of Theology, Holistic Ministry, and Public Policy, Palmer Seminary at Eastern University

First Chronicles 12:32 mentions the sons of Issachar, who "understood the times and knew what God's people should do." Of course, one cannot understand our times without going into the past and realizing the roots of our current historical situation. Our brave authors here do this for us, helping us learn things we did not know, underscoring certain features of our past social failings and bad theologies, and then offer insightful theological reflections to help us name sin, seek forgiveness and move forward in newness of life. Anyone wanting to be Christ's ambassadors of reconciliation and agents of God's transforming kingdom simply must grapple with the social sins named in this book, nurturing hearts that can become broken and healed by these stories of pain and compromise. We must learn the rhythms and goodness of grace that comes through lament and admitting guilt. This book will indeed help us be sons and daughters of Issachar—aware, repentant, wise, and relevant. I pray it gets a wide, wide readership.

Byron K. Borger, Hearts & Minds Bookstore

Reading *Forgive Us* was an experience I'd never had with any other book: though I expected it to be the kind I'd want to put down immediately—*because it would be the kind that convicted me*—I couldn't put it down. Not only did I not want to put it down, at the end of the first chapter I wanted to leap ahead and read each new chapter *simultaneously!* It's *that good.*

Like many, I recognize the besetting sins of the church today. But this rich exploration into the history and motivations for our sin was a meaty feast, helping me to understand the *reasons* we've behaved as we have and fueling my own passion to embrace relationships that are truly patterned after the person of Jesus. I thank these wise, brave authors for the leadership they're providing today with their ministries and with this book. In these pages Christ's bride is being equipped for faithful living.

Margot Starbuck, author of *Permission Granted: Learning to Live Graciously among Sinners and Saints*

The authors' generous hearts help open us to the difficult, prophetic truths they have to share. Aside from looking back on historical transgressions, they challenge us to do the necessary work of confession and reconciliation for the sinfulness in our midst, here and now, both individually and as church. The real gift is that it is through this humble search for forgiveness that we find the opportunity for real healing in a fractured, skeptical world.

Christian Piatt, author of *PostChristian* and *Blood Doctrine*

In fidelity to the way of Jesus, this collection of prophetic writings is an urgent call to repentance and confession not just for evangelicals but for every Christian denomination and institution. "Woe to you rich.... "(Luke 6:24–26). Do we dare confess the intrinsic evil of the invisible structures of excessive wealth while billions of people live on less than a dollar a day, of the manufactures of weapons of war and destruction, of industry that is devastating the environment, of developers who are destroying indigenous peoples for the sake of development? The authors of this book write for today with the same fire, clarity, and depth of the great prophets of the Bible.

Rev. Dr. Virgilio Elizondo, Professor of Hispanic and Pastoral Theology University of Notre Dame

forgive us

Mae Elise Cannon
(Senior Director of Advocacy and Outreach, World Vision US)

Social Justice Handbook:
Small Steps for a Better World (IVP, 2009)

Just Spirituality:
How Faith Practices Fuel Social Action (IVP, 2012)

Lisa Sharon Harper
(Senior Director of Mobilizing, Sojourners)

Evangelical Does Not Equal Republican ... or Democrat
(The New Press, 2008)

Left, Right, and Christ: Evangelical Faith in Politics,
co-authored with D.C. Innes (Elevate, 2012)

An Push da Wind Down: A Play in Two Acts
(Samuel French, 1995)

Troy Jackson
(Executive Director of the Amos Project
and Co-Director of Ohio Prophetic Voices)

Becoming King: Martin Luther King Jr.
and the Making of a National Leader
(University Press of Kentucky Press, 2008)

The Papers of Martin Luther King Jr., Vol. VI:
Advocate of the Social Gospel,
co-editor (University of California Press, 2007)

Soong-Chan Rah
(Milton B. Engebretson Professor of Church Growth
and Evangelism, North Park Theological Seminary)

The Next Evangelicalism: Freeing the Church
from Western Cultural Captivity (IVP, 2009)

Many Colors: Cultural Intelligence
for a Changing Church (Moody, 2010)

Honoring the Generations:
Learning with Asian North American Congregations,
co-editor (Judson, 2012)

forgive us

confessions of a compromised faith

MAE ELISE CANNON

LISA SHARON HARPER

TROY JACKSON

SOONG-CHAN RAH

ZONDERVAN®

ZONDERVAN

Forgive Us
Copyright © 2014 by Soong-Chan Rah, Mae Elise Cannon, Lisa Sharon Harper,
Troy Jackson

This title is also available as a Zondervan ebook.
Visit www.zondervan.com/ebooks.

Requests for information should be addressed to:
Zondervan, 3900 Sparks Dr. SE, Grand Rapids, Michigan 49546

Library of Congress Cataloging-in-Publication Data

     Forgive us : confessions of a compromised faith / Mae Elise Cannon, Lisa
Sharon Harper, Troy Jackson, Soong-Chan Rah.
       pages   cm
     ISBN 978-0-310-51596-8
     1. United States—Church history. 2. Christianity—United States. 3.
Laments—United States. 4. Confession. 5. Sins. 6. Repentance. 7. Forgiveness
of sin. I. Cannon, Mae Elise, 1976– joint author.
     BR515.F64 2014
     277.3'0083—dc23   2014013948

Cover design: *Michelle Lenger*
Cover photography: *Masterfile*
Interior design: *David Conn*
Edited by: *Madison Trammel, Kelsey Kaemingk, and Bob Hudson*

Printed in the United States of America

14 15 16 17 18 19 20 21 22 23 24 /DCI/ 20 19 18 17 16 15 14 13 12 11 10 9 8 7 6 5 4 3 2 1

This book is dedicated
to Dr. Richard Twiss,
friend, brother, mentor, and guide.
—From "All Your Relations"

People of faith have lost their moral authority ... because they have lacked humility: they have failed to acknowledge the ways they are part of the problem.[1]

Ibrahim Abdul-Matin, policy advisor
in NYC Office of Long Term
Planning and Sustainability

If my people, who are called by my name, will humble themselves and pray and seek my face and turn from their wicked ways, then I will hear from heaven, and I will forgive their sin and will heal their land.

2 Chronicles 7:14

contents

foreword
by Dr. Mark Labberton
and Rev. Jim Wallis

Repentance and forgiveness are never finished. What they can be, and often are, however, is avoided or denied. Therein lies the tragic mistake of the church, the error that this book seeks to redress. The issue is not merely the frequent failure of the people of God, but our additional failure to admit fault and to seek forgiveness and reconciliation. Too often, the churches are very aware of the sins of others but quite unaware of our own.

No one comes to repentance and confession easily. That's the point, of course. It requires two things few of us like: taking responsibility and embracing a kind of death. This is not the good news we like living or proclaiming. But we must acknowledge our complicity or entanglement in systems and patterns of sin and injustice, and we must die to the illusion that such history can be escaped. If we are to mirror the new life that is the resurrection, dying precedes rising. Repentance and forgiveness precede reconciliation. And the biblical term for repentance is *metanoia*, which means to "turn around and go in a new direction."

Chapter by chapter, then, this team of authors walks Protestants, and particularly evangelicals, into some of our worst history. We are led through painful events and patterns, through the echoing rhetoric of self-serving, self-justifying theology used to rationalize bad, even abusive, practice. If we are honest, this book leaves us scorched by flames our very evangelicalism has often stoked.

The pain in this book that matters most, however, is not our smited conscience, but the legacy of wounds inflicted and intensified by our evangelical faith. Clearly, some of our worst sins have seriously hurt other people. The true suffering this book underlines is that of a world of God's Creation, and that of men and women — "a little lower than the angels" — that have been subjected to unjust and demeaning treatment, perpetrated and justified by some spurious attitudes and convictions held by much of the church. And all this still lingers. Its stench still affects the lives of many.

And yet, as evangelicals we are struck that our eagerness for new life and a new day presses us on and sometimes seems like a placard slapped onto painful wounds rather than the source of healing and transformation. When we fail to take seriously enough what our tribe has done to others, what its implications have been and are, and what steps are necessary to bring about reconciliation, we undermine the gospel we proclaim. The "good news" of the gospel is too often undermined by the bad news of evangelical behavior.

For some, this book may seem like wallowing or self-flagellation. We don't believe it is either, nor are either the intent of its authors. To go back and rehearse history, as painful as it may be, gives us the chance to face the actions and words of some that caused profound destruction in the lives of others. Then we enter a different space in which to live and love, serve and grow. Honest confession always allows new possibilities and responses to enter the scene.

Out of such remembrance can come true repentance, and out of such repentance the possibility of God's merciful reconciliation and healing. It is to this great end, through these deep waters, that we must pass. The demonstration that *Forgive Us* will have done its work will not be measured merely by sorrowful repentance nor by heartfelt liturgy. It will be made evident if it contributes to our sustained and humble pursuit of that communion with God and neighbor that remembers the past and that shows in our earnest dedication to live out the new humanity that is God's gift.

introduction

forgive us.
    Forgive us, God.
    Forgive us, world.
    Forgive us.

The authors of this book are evangelical Christians. As part of our identity we hold to a high view of Scripture's authority over our lives, we affirm the value of Christian community, and we take seriously our witness to the world. Like many, we look at our world and feel overwhelmed by the depth of individual, social, environmental, and systemic injustice. Ethnic, gender, national, class, and political warfare have shredded the notion of the common good in our society. Our tendency is to shift the blame, attributing such injustices to others or to the inescapable reality of a fallen world.

But if we are honest with ourselves we can see it. *We* are culpable. As Christians, we are guilty before God and before the world. God sees it. The world sees it—and because the world sees our sin and perceives that we have not removed the log from our own eye before calling out the specks in the eyes of others, our hypocrisy has been exposed. We have damaged our own witness to the world.

So we offer this book as a confession. We see our hypocrisy and we repent. Our unexamined and unconfessed history prevents our full expression of and witness to the Christian message. The eyes of our hearts have not been enlightened, which in turn hinders our ability to enlighten the eyes of others. Our witness should begin with our own testimony and the example of our confession, and it is our hope that these confessions will serve as a step forward in the healing process of our land as our wrongdoing is acknowledged and as more and more Christians follow the biblical model of personal and representational repentance.

The practice of confession is rooted in the Bible. The Scriptures consistently attest that confession and repentance are expected of those who have neglected and injured others and turned their backs on God. From the Hebrew Bible (what Christians refer to as "The Old Testament") through the Christian Scripture ("The New Testament"), Scripture repeatedly calls God's people to repent. Confession is the appropriate response to sinfulness. Given the evidence of our history, we call upon the American church, corporately, to respond with confession for our deeds and the deeds of our forebears.

Nehemiah

The story of Nehemiah offers an account of the power of corporate confession. When the book of Nehemiah opens, we find the prophet himself living a privileged life as cupbearer to Artaxerxes, the Persian king. The Jews had been forced into captivity in 599 BCE, nearly 160 years before Nehemiah's time. Even after forced Babylonian captivity had ended in 538 BCE, many Jews, including Nehemiah, chose to stay in exile.

Meanwhile, the walls of Jerusalem were ransacked and the city's gates were "burned with fire" (Nehemiah 1:3).

News of the sad state of the physical and social well-being of Nehemiah's people prompted him to examine their spiritual state. They had walked away from the commandments of God (1:7, 9:26). They did not honor the Sabbath (9:14–17), and without the Sabbath, merchants and nobles had license to pursue wealth unabated and exploit their workers. Likewise, the workers were tempted not to trust God for their livelihood but rather the pure sweat of their brows to earn their living. Without the Sabbath, foreign workers were particularly vulnerable to exploitation.

Nehemiah 5:1–11 tells how the nobles and policy makers were crushing the image of God on earth through the exploitation of their own people. As the leaders continued to disregard the Sabbath, the workers got no rest. They were overtaxed and had to pay so much interest that they had no food to eat. This forced them to give up their land, orchards, and homes for grain. The people were so desperate that they sold their sons and daughters into slavery, after which many of their daughters had suffered at the hands of the nobles who raped them.[2]

Nehemiah could have felt paralyzed by the gravity of this situation. He could have responded with apathy; after all, he was free of any immediate responsibility. Living in exile as he did, far from Jerusalem, he could have claimed innocence since he wasn't a part of that oppressive system. But he did none of the above.

Nehemiah understood the power of corporate confession. He confessed not only his own sins but the historic sins of his ancestors: "I confess the sins we Israelites, including myself and my father's family, have committed against you. We have acted very wickedly toward you. We have not obeyed the commands, decrees and laws you gave your servant Moses" (1:6–7).

He opened his heart to godly grief on behalf of the sins of his people, confessed them, then busied himself with doing what he could to make things right.

"When I heard these things, I sat down and wept. For some days I mourned and fasted and prayed before the God of heaven" (1:4). Through prayer and confession, Nehemiah allowed the Spirit of God to soften his heart. He acknowledged the repercussions of the feast of lies that the nobles and policy makers had been eating with respect to God, the people, and the land. Godly grief does not paralyze with a pervasive sense of guilt. Rather, it identifies specific ways we have turned from God and offers a holy opportunity for the restoration of relationship with God, others, and the land by reconnecting our hearts to God's heart and then to the hearts of those we have made to suffer. Godly grief leads to cleansing confession and repentance.

Godly confession tells the truth about God, about us, and about our actions. It tells the truth about the repercussions our actions have for us, our relationship with God, our families, others, the rest of creation, the systems that govern us, and life itself. Nehemiah tells the truth about God and his people:

> Lord, the God of heaven, the great and awesome God, who keeps his covenant of love with those who love him and keep his commandments, let your ear be attentive and your eyes open to hear the prayer your servant is praying before you day and night for your servants, the people of Israel. I confess the sins we Israelites, including myself and my father's family, have committed against you. (1:5–6)

What is the truth? God is more awesome than wealth!

What is the truth? God loves and provides for those who keep his commands.

What is the truth? The people of Israel have failed to keep God's commandments, statutes, and policies.

What is the truth? "Both I and my family have sinned," said Nehemiah.

He had not grown up in Jerusalem, but he took personal responsibility for the sins of his people living there. He exercised representational repentance by standing in the gap, offering prayers on behalf of his people.

For Nehemiah it was not enough to pray. Godly lament and confession should lead to repentance, and repentance requires an about-face in our actions and a deep change in our way of life. Repentance led Nehemiah to leave the king's court, forgo comfort and security, and do everything he could to rebuild the walls, restore the gates, and establish a thriving Jerusalem whose people lived according to the commands of God. Nehemiah recognized that the spiritual adultery of his people manifested itself in systemic, social evil. Repentance could not stop on a spiritual level; it had to be worked out in people's lives and ultimately manifested in systemic, social change. Nehemiah provided an example of public leadership concerning public issues. It became a part of Nehemiah's confession.

Nehemiah lived at the whim of a single king whose word was law. In our modern democratic society the equivalent to King Artaxerxes' edicts would be the policies and laws of our school boards, city councils, state assemblies, and Congress. It would include the policy agendas of our mayors, governors, and presidents. Public leadership took Nehemiah to the king, just as public leadership might take us to the office of our city council members, our US senator, or even to the White House. Public leadership requires that we confront the full range of principalities and powers — Wall Street, Madison Avenue, multinational corporations, the prison industrial complex, and many others.

Such leadership may also take us to the feet of those we have exploited. Like Nehemiah, we must return to the breached city. We must examine the land and, as Nehemiah did (Nehemiah

5 and 9), join hands with those who have suffered and call out the oppressors to cease their oppression. The people of the breach know what needs to be rebuilt. The people of the breach know best how to rebuild it. So what is Nehemiah's role? To repent. And repentance allows us to partner with the people of the breach to supply needed resources to create the climate for deep cultural, social, and systemic transformation.

Poets and Prophets

One of the most crucial but neglected modes of prayer in the Bible is the lament. A lament, as offered by poets and prophets in the Hebrew Scriptures, required the recognition of the reality of one's suffering and the offering of a petition trusting in YHWH's judgment and appropriate response. A lament acknowledges reality and the necessity of repentance in response to that reality. A lament is the response of suffering humanity to God and the acknowledgement of God's sovereignty in the midst of that suffering. It eschews quick solutions and simple answers and seeks to embrace the reality of suffering with a greater dependence upon God.

While prominent and even essential in the Scriptures, the lament is conspicuously absent in American Christianity. It is underrepresented in our liturgical traditions and church hymnals, and conspicuously absent in our collections of contemporary worship songs. The absence of laments may be attributable to several key factors, one of which is certainly the triumphalism and exceptionalism that all too often mark the American church.

The church tends to view itself as the world's problem solver. We think of ourselves as the ones who will end global inequality and injustice. This belief in the unique calling of the American church to fix the problems of the world results in a diminishing of, or a blindness to, lament and the necessary confession that is inherent within it. When the church sees itself in this way, it fails to recognize what at times is its own faulty, culturally captive, and dysfunctional theology. The American church often chooses to ignore its own tainted history and move too quickly toward offering solutions for everyone else's problems.

Our selective memory causes us to think we can solve world hunger through Western cultural imperialism, when the imperialism of previous generations was the source of much of the poverty in the contemporary world. The American tendency toward hyper-individualism, materialism, and triumphalism has infected the church more than we often realize, and that may be why the church is impotent in dealing with issues of global justice. Why call on God for help when we think we don't really need any help? The absence of an ongoing practice of lament and confession in the church exacerbates its grandiose assumptions of exceptionalism rather than evoking the necessary humility. Why engage in humble confession when we assume we have nothing to confess? The reality check that confession demands is absent, leading to the perpetuation of sinful attitudes and values.

The Scriptures testify to the importance of lament. Nearly 40 percent of the Psalms are laments. A quick glance through the Christian Copyright International's list reveals that less than 10 percent of those songs would even remotely qualify as laments.[3] Our worship does not match the biblical testimony. The Hebrew Scriptures offer a significant number of communal laments that point to a corporate responsibility and a corporate sense of culpability. The book of Psalms provides numerous examples of laments offered on behalf of the entire community. While many are spoken in a personal and individual voice, they reflect the feelings of the larger community.

In the book of Lamentations, for example, a lament is

offered in chapter 3 by someone identified as the "strong man."[4] This man observes the destruction of Jerusalem and offers a lament and confession on behalf of God's people. In all likelihood, the strong man reflects the voice of Jeremiah, who offers a lament even though he is the only innocent leader among God's people at the time. Jeremiah had repeatedly done what was right before the Lord and had provided faithful witness up until the moment of Jerusalem's destruction. Jeremiah, however, is willing to take on the sins of his entire community and offer an individual lament that reflects the feelings of that community. A corporate confession is offered by one individual without fault.

The poetic and prophetic passages in the Bible testify to the importance of confession, and this confession is never limited to the personal and the private. Laments and confessions are offered on behalf of the whole community, revealing an understanding in Hebrew culture of the corporate nature of prayer.

The Teachings of Jesus

The Gospels also testify to the importance of individual and corporate confession. Jesus' teachings about the kingdom provide an important foundation for corporate confession. In the Sermon on the Mount, Jesus describes the value system of the kingdom of God and how it differs from the world's system of values. Instead of responding with violence, we are called upon to turn the other cheek. Instead of the powerful and triumphant being rewarded in heaven, the poor, the mourners, and the meek are the ones who are blessed.

Jesus raises the standard of behavior for his followers. We are not to follow the patterns of the world any longer, but rather the higher standard of Christ's kingdom. It is the expectation and responsibility of every follower of Jesus to do the right thing even when others do not. Our current cultural context elevates the self and fails to acknowledge human sinfulness. Evangelicals often fault modern American society for its inability to deal effectively with the reality of sin. Twenty-first century evangelicals spend an extraordinary amount of time pointing out the sins evident in the culture. But instead of doing that, couldn't the church make the confession of its own sins a higher priority? The church could model a countercultural practice of confession, reflecting kingdom values rather than worldly ones. Jesus' teaching about a countercultural value system should lead us to the realization of our own human fallenness and to the subsequent act of confession.

Confession arises out of the countercultural context of God's kingdom. At the same time, Jesus' teaching points to the collective, corporate nature of human fallenness. When Jesus addressed Nicodemus, he pointed out that "God so loved the *world* ..." (John 3:16, emphasis added). The Greek word for *world* is *cosmos*, which not only implies every individual, but also the corporate systems and structures of the whole world.[5] *Cosmos* cannot be understood simply as a way to engage sin on a personal level. God's love for the world should not be reduced only to his love for individuals. Instead, *cosmos* implies the work of Jesus in the collective meaning of the word: *the world*. When John the Baptist acknowledged Jesus as the one "who takes away the sin of the world" (John 1:29), he used the same word — *cosmos*. It expresses the idea that Jesus' salvific work applies to all humanity.

Our hyper-individualized culture wants to read the Gospels strictly through the lens of the individual: "Jesus loves *me*," "Jesus died for *my* sins," "Jesus died on the cross for *me*." Of course the love of Jesus is clearly and fully expressed to the individual, but it is not limited to the individual. God's act of loving the *cosmos*, and Jesus' task of taking away the sins of that *cosmos*, mean that sin can be understood in a corporate sense. A confession of sin, therefore, can be a corporate expression. Corporate confession challenges us to see beyond our individualistic, Western worldview. It recognizes that sin operates collectively, and that the responsibility of the church as a whole is to recognize that it too has sinned collectively.

Pauline Epistles

The apostle Paul also points to the importance of confession. He reminds the church that "all have sinned and fall short of the glory of God" (Romans 3:23). We are all equal in our sinfulness. Even as a Pharisee descended from Pharisees (Acts 23:6), Paul considered himself to be "the worst of sinners" (1 Timothy 1:16). No individual is without sin. Paul repeatedly asserts the universality of sin for all of humanity.

Because all have sinned, to deny culpability is fruitless. Most evangelicals acknowledge that every person has sinned, but evangelicals often fail to recognize that sin exists well beyond the personal level. Paul's emphasis on the universality of sin suggests that we should also be aware of the power of corporate sin. Nowhere, in fact, does Scripture ever reject the idea of corporate sin, and yet we frequently find just such rejection in the history of the evangelical church in America. In the nineteenth century, Christianity often found a balance between personal evangelism and social justice (for example, in the work of the Salvation Army and the commitment of many Christians to work for the abolition of slavery), but early in the twentieth century, American fundamentalists and evangelicals shifted their emphasis heavily toward individualistic expressions of faith. They separated personal evangelism from social justice. Historian David Moberg identifies this shift as "the Great Reversal."[6] Twentieth-century evangelicalism witnessed the transition from a holistic understanding of the gospel to a more reductionist individual expression. Paul's words would be reduced to refer merely to personal rather than corporate sin.

Jesus, however, came for the entire spectrum of human sinfulness. For American Christianity to focus exclusively on the personal nature of Jesus' work on the cross actually diminishes that work. Western culture's focus on the redemption of the individual prevents our engagement with other forms of sin, reducing Jesus to a purely personal God. In Ephesians, Paul demonstrates that spiritual power is at work in the prayer life of the believer. He prays for the Ephesians "to know this love that surpasses knowledge—that you may be filled to the measure of all the fullness of God" (Ephesians 3:19). Paul's intercessory prayer reminds us that God "is able to do immeasurably more than all we ask or imagine, according to his power that is at work within us" (3:20). Why would the church want to limit that power to the realm of personal sin only and not call upon God's power to work in all realms?

Forgive Us

Around the world, many people have grown angry and frustrated with organized religion—and with evangelical Christianity in particular. Too often the church has proven a source of pain rather than a place of hope. This book, *Forgive Us*, acknowledges the legitimacy of much of that anger and recognizes that the church through the ages has experienced significant brokenness, a brokenness that demands to be acknowledged and repented of. This book focuses specifically on the history of the Christian church in the United States and the role it has played in many tragic and harmful events.

In chapter 1, we examine environmental degradation and our failure to properly steward God's creation. In chapter 2, we look at the history of the genocide of the indigenous people in the Americas and the church's culpability in this shameful act. Chapter 3 explores the historical sin of racism and the theological roots of modern-day racism. Chapter 4 discusses the ongoing oppression of women and the sinful justification of sexism in the church. Chapter 5 tackles the church's marginalization and abuse of the LGBTQ community. Chapter 6 explores the sin of nativism and the corresponding acts of sin committed against immigrants. Chapter 7 examines Christian religion-centric assumptions and the accompanying historically sinful actions of the church against the Jewish and Muslim communities.

Many Christians today are unaware of the events that mark the American church's greatest tragedies. In *Forgive Us*, we seek to provide brief, accurate, and compelling histories of some of the church's greatest shortcomings. Each chapter will offer a historical analysis of a situation that needs to be confessed, because awareness is critical in the process of true repentance. After each analysis, we offer biblical and theological reflections on the historical issue. Each chapter closes with appropriate confession, repentance, and ways for us to move forward (including positive models of the church offering confession) that will promote peace, justice, and reconciliation. When apologies without knowledge are offered, individually or on behalf of the church, they are anemic at best. When the church has a holistic understanding of its failings, repentance is the appropriate response. This book seeks to serve as a church's confession and to engage with the surrounding culture by issuing a heartfelt request for forgiveness and a new beginning.

Our goal is that these reflections will expose the lies the church has believed about God, the people, and the land. At the end of each chapter, we include invitations to reflect, lament, and agree with God that lies are lies. We invite you to consider how these lies have affected our nation, our cities, our families, and our lives. And we invite you to join both the Hebrew prophets and the saints throughout the ages in prayers of confession and acts of repentance.

The four authors who contributed to this book strongly believe that the church must recognize the truth of its history before it can move forward toward forgiveness, reconciliation, and peace. This book is our confession and our call to repentance. The authors are African American, European American, and Asian American. We are women and men. We are environmentally conscious and environmental over-consumers. We have means and we have less. The one thing we most have in common is our faith. We are evangelicals. As such, we share a common historical, theological, liturgical, and social heritage—one that we want to honor. But we also recognize aspects of our life together that reveal deep complicity with and responsibility for evil. With our confessions we follow the example of Nehemiah, the challenge of the Hebrew prophets and poets, the teachings of Jesus, and the insights of the apostle Paul. We seek to count ourselves among those who stand in the gap, proclaiming the truth about God, others, and our land. We invite you to join us.

If you are a Christian, join us on a journey through truth and lies, godly grief, confession, and repentance. With each step—and with each tear, prayer, and tangible act of love—we pray that God might restore the walls of our cities, nation, and world.

If you are not a Christian, hear our prayer: "Forgive us."

CHAPTER 1

sins against God's creation

Historical Reflection

Well-meaning Christians have different interpretations of the science surrounding today's environmental concerns. They often disagree about how the Bible and Christian theology speak to a Christ follower's moral responsibility in stewarding creation and responding to environmental needs. Some see technological advancement as an appropriate way for humanity to bring glory to God. Others assert that the environment and creation should be approached with greater sensitivity and an ever-growing understanding of environmental justice on behalf of the kingdom of the Creator. This chapter reviews some of the historical perspectives of American Christians toward the stewardship of the environment and creation in North America.

European settlers imported their faith to the Americas in

ways that often had a negative impact on the environment. Otsego settlers in New York, inspired by their Protestant faith, believed that "conquering the forest and its wild animals was a service to God."[1] These early colonists believed stewardship of the creation meant conquering the unredeemed landscape and destroying whatever was dangerous, including wild animals. Society at that time gave special honor to settlers who destroyed such beasts as wolves, panthers, and bears.[2] Settlers encouraged the killing of wild animals in part because of their need for safety and security, but an excessive destruction of wildlife was not only commonplace but lauded in early Colonial American society. According to historian Alan Taylor, early settlers "assailed the wild plant and animal life with a vengeance born, in part, from the memory of recent sufferings," and thus, deforestation, as one manifestation, became a mark of pride and status.[3] The conditions were harsh, and mere survival was part of the daily struggle for many colonists. As Protestant Christians, most of them saw their transformation of the forest as creating permanent communities and a fulfillment of their religious duty rather than an abuse of the landscape.

In a highly debated essay about the environment, "The Trouble with Wilderness, or, Getting Back to the Wrong Nature," renowned historian William Cronon writes about the deep roots of the "wilderness ethic" in American history. Before the eighteenth century, the word *wilderness* had largely negative connotations, often denoting hostility—such connotations as *deserted, savage, desolate, barren*—all words used to describe the early American settlers' experience of the wilderness.[4] This explains some of the hostility toward vegetation, nature, and the animal kingdom.

Furthermore, Cronon asserts that the origin of the colonists' views were significantly informed by the King James Version of the Bible. Such verses as Genesis 1:28 became powerful justifications for the settlers: "Replenish the earth, and subdue it: and have dominion over the fish of the sea, and over the fowl of the air, and over every living thing that moveth upon the earth."

Of course some early Christian settlers viewed the continent's vast resources as a manifestation of God's creative power and believed the abundance surrounding them to be worthy of appreciation and praise. Still, their wonder was balanced against such biblical accounts as Moses' forty years of wandering and Christ's temptation by Satan — events that occurred in "the wilderness."[5] According to Cronon, "Wilderness ... was a place to which one came only against one's will, and always in fear and trembling."[6] The wilderness, in early American Christian thought, was where God conquered the sinful nature of man, the devil was overcome, and temptations were faced by the triumphant nature of Christ. Thus, the wilderness had little inherent value other than needing to be conquered and overcome.

The religious obligation that some early colonists felt to subdue the animal kingdom continued well into the nineteenth century. Antebellum Americans took seriously their perceived commitments to conquer nature and often recorded their conquests as a mark of pride and a sign of victory. In 1850 one old hunter in New York "calculated that in his lifetime he had killed 77 panthers, 214 wolves, 219 bears, and 2,550 deer."[7] Animals were not always killed for such practical reasons as protection, food, or the use of their fur or hides; rather they continued to be viewed as "beasts of the field" whose destruction was an expression of the power and "dominion" of man, as an agent of God, over creation. Little did they know that by killing the most dangerous predators, like wolves, those lower on the food chain, like deer, were able to overpopulate, which caused disease and other problems by throwing the local ecosystem off balance.

While eighteenth-century Americans perceived nature and the wilderness as "the antithesis of all that was orderly and good," as Cronon puts it, this notion began to shift with the rise of the Romantic movement in the decades following the establishment of the United States of America.[8] The possibility of viewing the wilderness as somehow sacred had been present even when Europeans settled the Americas; however, this attitude became more widely adopted in the nineteenth century. Cronon asserts there were now fewer perceived boundaries between the human and the nonhuman, between the material and supernatural worlds, than when the settlers first pondered the idea of wilderness.[9] As communities grew more stable, the need to overcome the evil forces of the wilderness diminished, and the redeemable qualities of nature began to be acknowledged and admired.

In the first half of the nineteenth century, as Romanticism continued to spread, American Christians came to be strongly influenced by the movement's idea of the *sublime*. The *sublime* refers to whatever is otherworldly, beyond human comprehension, reflecting a power and grandeur that could even be supernatural in origin. Christians who viewed nature as sublime began to view animals and plants as divine expressions of God's manifestation on earth. Rather than being viewed as evil, creation became increasingly understood as a doorway to the divine. For Christians, God's presence began to be increasingly associated with nature. They came to see and experience God in natural phenomena such as mountains, fields, valleys, and rivers, and also in natural acts of creation such as the sunrise, storms, the wind, and waves.[10]

This view of nature was deeply influenced by the writings of Henry David Thoreau, Ralph Waldo Emerson, and James Fenimore Cooper, among others. Their romantic ideologies challenged the assumption that wilderness was a force that needed to be overcome. Cronon writes of this phenomenon, "Wilderness fulfills the old romantic project of secularizing Judeo-Christian values so as to make a new cathedral not in some petty human building but in God's own creation, Nature itself." [11] Wilderness came to be associated with the natural order of things and goodness, like the Garden of Eden itself. This shift in Christian thinking had a powerful impact on Americans' views of the environment.

By the late nineteenth century, the United States government had begun to establish the first national parks, including Yosemite, Yellowstone, and Mackinac National Park. Following this momentum, Theodore Roosevelt was the first American president to make conservation a prime campaign issue for his administration. In 1906 he signed a bill that consolidated the control of Yosemite National Park under the ownership, management, and regulation of the federal government. A decade later the National Parks Service was established.[12]

In the twentieth century, this attitude of awe and admiration for the environment shifted to a modernist framework, stressing utility and functionality. The country's vast open lands came to be thought of as a direct gift from God, providing abundant natural resources—coal, natural gas, minerals, or other products. This new theological emphasis focused on "stewardship"; that is, the land provided resources that God intended humans to exploit. It was not only a privilege but an obligation for Christians to use and steward those resources by securing the greatest value from them.

This shifting idea of Christian stewardship had devastating effects, however, in regions such as Appalachia which are often characterized by their extreme poverty. By the 1960s, government programs such as the War on Poverty were significantly engaged in Appalachia. That program was part of President Johnson's Great Society, which endorsed the goal of ending domestic poverty. Many economists viewed such poverty as a "deviation from the norm" and believed it could be eliminated by continued growth and economic development — in other words, by even more effective stewardship of the earth.[13]

Two predominant assumptions influenced the development of Appalachia and the significant poverty that was, and continues to be, significant throughout the region. First, Appalachia was viewed "as a place of cultural backwardness in a nation of progressive values." Many people believed that the region's poverty was the result of "cultural deficiencies, antiquated values, and low expectations."[14] In other words, poverty was not the result of outside forces, but the outcome of fundamental deficiencies in the people themselves and their communities. Christian leaders supported this view, often identifying the people of the Appalachia as "backward" and ill-prepared for the modern world. Jack Weller, a Presbyterian minister from New York, summed it up: "The greatest challenge of Appalachia, and the most difficult ... is its people."[15]

To address this perceived backwardness, missionary efforts were aimed at the region and became an integral part of the area's history since the late nineteenth century. Catholic and Protestant groups alike sent young people as teachers, ministers, and social workers. While many of these efforts brought about significant progress in the lives of individuals, they failed to address systemic economic issues affecting the community. Religious workers, guided by the belief that the people of the Appalachia were the problem, sought to help them "pull themselves up by the boot straps" while at the same time failing to address holistic issues of societal transformation.[16]

A second predominant assumption was that Appalachia, like the rest of America, would become more productive and successful if it was only subjected to more technology and industrial advancement. Again, this ideology was deeply rooted in the notion from Genesis that people could best steward God's creation by subduing it. Historian Ronald Eller writes in his book *Uneven Ground: Appalachia since 1945* about this phenomenon:

> As a result of the rapid expansion of modern technologies after World War II, difficult terrain could be breached to promote commerce with the larger world. Streams could be relocated, rivers damned, and hillsides developed for housing, recreation, and business use. Most of all, entire mountains and ranges of mountains could be leveled to extract their mineral resources and to create a landscape more suitable for manufacturing and retail expansion.[17]

Often the exploitation of the land for natural resources did not directly benefit the community, instead creating cycles of dependency in which local workers were paid minimum wage, subjugated to poor working conditions, and could do little as their social systems became increasingly dependent on the corporations that controlled the industries. This dominance of industrial influence even extended to the local churches, which were themselves largely dependent on a company's financial support.[18]

In the 1960s and 1970s significant national movements began, particularly in Appalachia, against strip mining. Support for a national ban on surface mining reached its peak in 1972 with the Buffalo Creek crisis in Logan County, West Virginia. Over the span of several years, the Buffalo Mining Company, a subsidiary of Pittston Coal Company, the largest independent coal producer in the US, had placed dams along Buffalo Creek as a means of waste disposal. These came to be known as "gob pile dams" because they appeared to be black pools located in the middle fork of Buffalo Creek. They consisted of rock debris, dirt, and other waste discharged from coal plants. These dump sites are still so common that locals often use regional slang to identify them: "colliery spoil" (if you are

British), "culm" (if you are from Pennsylvania), and "Red Dog" (if the gob pile has caught fire and is burning).[19] On February 26, 1972, one gob pile dam broke, causing a thirty-foot wave of water to descend upon a nearby town, killing 125 people and leaving more than 4,000 homeless.[20] According to Eller, Pittston Coal Company assumed no responsibility for the tragedy. One company representative even declared that the tragedy was "an act of God."[21]

Sadly, the Christian community often does not respond to tragedies like the Buffalo Creek disaster. Only a few young radical Christians, such as Michael Clark of the Church of the Brethren Appalachian Caucus and the Reverend B. Lloyd of the Anglican Appalachian People's Service Organization, took up the cause. Clark and Lloyd believed that the degradation of the environment was the result of the exploitation of workers in their community. One activist wrote: "People are forced out of their homes and from their farms because it is more profitable to let mud slide into living rooms and across cornfields than it is to mine coal with care. Little thought is given to farmlands which would have fed families for generations to come."[22]

By the 1970s and 1980s, poor communities in the region, including Native American and African American communities, "began to notice that toxic mining and dumping on their lands by deregulated industries were causing elevated levels of cancer and other life-threatening ailments."[23] The effects of industrialization and strip mining were having a devastating effect on the people living alongside these projects of so-called advancement. While many Christians remained silent, the United Church of Christ sponsored a study in 1987 called "Toxic Waste and Race," which found a direct correlation between the placement of toxic dumping sites and poor communities of color.[24] This study was a step in the right direction, tracing the links between poverty, race, and environmental degradation. In the 1990s, following in the footsteps of the "Toxic Waste and Race" report, the environmental justice movement was born. New environmental legislation, such as the Clean Air Act of 1990, was a direct outcome of this movement and highlighted the growing emphasis for community well-being to be addressed holistically in light of proper treatment of the environment and the earth's resources.

All these stories, from the early colonists' excessive slaughter of wild animals to the Buffalo Creek tragedy, shed light on how Christian attitudes have created a climate in which sins against creation take place. Christians have not only sinned against the environment, but they have also failed to intervene when environmental degradation is perpetuated by their neighbors and others in society. In fact, because Christians often benefit financially from the very industries that have devastated God's creation, they are often those industries' strongest allies and supporters.

In the late 1990s, Vice President Al Gore became an outspoken voice on behalf of the environment. His 2006 documentary, *An Inconvenient Truth*, sought to educate people about the negative effects of climate change. Many prominent Christians had a heyday criticizing not only the film, but attacking Gore and his efforts personally. For example, the policy arm of Dr. James Dobson's *Focus on the Family*, "Citizen Link," published several articles seeking to discredit Gore's message. One article, titled "A Skeptics Guide to Debunking Global Warming Alarmism" seeks to refute "catastrophe climate fears presented by the media, the United Nations, and former Vice President turned-foreign-lobbyist Al Gore."[25] Indeed, legitimate scientific reasons may well exist to counter some of Al Gore's assertions, especially as new research is done that refines and expands what we know. But some Christians seem to throw the baby out with the bathwater by rejecting all reasonable environmental concerns simply because such concerns are seen to be associated with liberal politics or are raised by people who do not share Christians' assumptions and principles.

One of the greatest concerns of twenty-first-century environmentalists is the overconsumption of the earth's resources, particularly by people in the US. With this in mind, Michael Northcott, a Christian ethicist and theologian, sheds light on the intersection between the environment and Christian ethics. He points out the current realities of the earth's environmental crisis: global warming, pollution, soil erosion, deforestation, species extinction, overpopulation, and overconsumption. In his book *The Environment and Christian Ethics*, Northcott calls on Christians to acknowledge the biological limits of our planet and the ways certain Christian assumptions and theological assertions have led to the abuse and injustice toward God's creation. Northcott asserts a Christian ethic that assumes "only the recovery of a spiritual, moral, and cosmological awareness of our place in the natural order ... can enable our civilization to begin to shift priorities and its values in a more harmonious direction."[26]

According to Northcott, one of the greatest responsibilities of North Americans, Christians included, is to deal with the excessive consumption of an unreasonable proportion of nature's limited resources and the production of an unconscionable amount of global pollution and waste.[27] Consider, for example, that the average person in the United States consumes 320 gallons (roughly 1,200 liters) of water per day, 30 percent of which is used for outside use such as watering the lawn or garden.[28] According to the World Health Organization, only 50 to 100 liters of water per day per person is required to meet basic hygiene and health needs around the world.[29] Christians must be willing to repent not only of our own overconsumption, but we must also ask forgiveness for those times when we do not intervene or speak out in response to the depletion of the earth's resources by corporations, institutions, and individuals.

Northcott paints a picture of how Christians could contribute to a solution:

> The central ecological virtue remains that of justice, for without a witness to justice it is doubtful that parish churches or any other kind of Christian community can be said to be places of good news to those who are excluded from the riches of the North, and for those animals and plants, fish and rivers, mountains and lakes, oceans and wilderness, whose beauty, order and fecundity is every day threatened by the advancing juggernaut of modern consumerism.[30]

In the twenty-first century, American Christians have experienced a boom of interest in nature, the environment, and what it means to be a good steward of creation. Christian books such as Jonathan Merritt's *Green Like God*, Ben Lowe's *Green Revolution*, Randy Woodley's *Shalom and the Community of Creation: An Indigenous Vision*, and Tri Robinson's *Saving God's Green Earth* were added to the library of resources calling Christians toward a new way of treating the environment. Christian environmentalists have outlined a theological framework to clarify Christians' responsibility to embrace the biblical mandate to care for creation. Resting on the belief that "God is green," Jonathan Merritt asserts that there are two types of divine revelation: the first is Scripture; and the second is the "general revelation we receive through nature."[31] Most followers of Christ believe this, but Christian activists like Merritt encourage people to live in a radically different way and to make changes that will have a lasting impact on the earth and our environment.

For Merritt, it is imperative that Christians integrate a theology of creation care in the way we live our lives each day. He provides practical examples, such as "turn off the juice" (switching the lights off when leaving a room), replacing incandescent bulbs with compact fluorescent ones, and other simple steps that reflect concern and care for creation in our daily choices.[32]

Theological Reflection

A certain kind of groaning comes from down deep in the bones, the kind that sounds as if a person is trying to push something toxic out of the body, trying to bring to the surface something that has been buried beneath a façade of wellness. This kind of groaning reveals a person (or a whole people) who is just hanging on until things are right again. These groans flow out of a deep grief and profound longing. Something has been lost— something very good.

Recently a woman named Barbara Brown retired after decades of service to Intervarsity Christian Fellowship. Her job was to pray. That's it. She was paid to pray. Once at a conference for black students from all parts of the African diaspora (including Africa, the US, the Caribbean, and Europe), the topic of the trans-Atlantic slave trade came up. Speakers analyzed the effects of the trade and talked about the havoc it wreaked on the people who were snatched, the people who were left behind, the land itself, and the nations that were pilfered. The panelists talked among themselves, and as they did so Barbara discerned that the group needed to stop talking and start praying.

So a special prayer session was added to the schedule. As it began, Barbara stepped forward and in her soft voice began to explain that there is a kind of prayer that bypasses words and connects directly to the heart of God. It is the prayer of lament, the prayer of longing. It is the same kind of prayer that Paul refers to in Romans 8:26 when he says: "In the same way, the Spirit helps us in our weakness. We do not know what we ought to pray for, but the Spirit himself intercedes for us through wordless groans." Barbara called it "groaning prayer."

The conference attendees sat silently as Barbara began to pray; first with the words "Oh, God! Heal us of the stifling effects of loss, never given the chance to be truly grieved! Help us to see ourselves as you see us—to imagine a world where we are seen by all as you see us."

Not long into Barbara's prayer one student groaned ... then another ... and another. Within minutes, the room heaved as this generation lamented the trauma, loss, fear, and humiliation that the trans-Atlantic slave trade had levied on nearly ten generations of their ancestors. Through their cries these students dared to imagine a world where they, their parents and grandparents, and their descendants might be healed.

In his letter to the Romans, Paul comforts the church by writing, "I consider that our present sufferings are not worth comparing with the glory that will be revealed in us. For the creation waits in eager expectation for the children of God to be revealed" (Romans 8:18–19). Paul had explained earlier in the letter that the "children of God" are those whose spirits cry "Father" when calling upon God. "For," according to Paul, "those who are led by the Spirit of God are the children of God" (Romans 8:14).

Consider this: What do children do? They identify with and follow their parents, literally and figuratively. They do as their parents do. So, the children of God that Paul speaks of not only say they are God's children, but they also do as God does. They are "led" by God. Why, then, is creation longing for the children of God to be revealed?

In Genesis 1, at the end of the sixth day of God's creative process, the Hebrew writer of this classically structured epic poem states that "God saw everything that he had made, and indeed, it was very good." The Hebrew words for "very good" are *tobe mehode*. *Tobe* means "good," but in the Hebrew context it not only refers to the state of the object itself but also to the interconnectedness of things—the ties that bind creation together. *Mehode* is an adjective meaning "forcefully" or "vehemently." To provide even more nuance to *mehode*'s meaning in Genesis 1, biblical scholar Terry McGonigal, in an email interview, added the words "abundant, flourishing, overflowing, never ending" to that list.

McGonigal further explained that the Hebrew term *tobe* appears by itself six times in the first chapter of Genesis—meaning just "good" without any qualifier. Then in 1:31, in the book's seventh use of that word, *tobe* is suddenly modified by the adjective *mehode*. McGonigal explained that the seventh use of any term is significant in Hebrew culture. The numbers 7 and 10 are the numbers for perfection. McGonigal concluded, "God is delighting in the totality of all creation in Genesis 1:31, the interconnected web of relationships now complete."

So when God looked around at the end of the sixth day and said "This is very good" what the original Hebrew readers would have gleaned in their cultural context was that each part of God's creation was not just good, but that the relationships between things were *forcefully* good, *abundantly* good, *vehemently* good, *overflowing* with goodness!

We were created, in other words, as part of a web of relationships. For instance, we were created for a relationship with God. Men and women were created for a relationship with each other. Humanity was created to exist in community—the first community consisting, arguably, of God, the man, and the woman. And humanity was created for a relationship with the rest of creation. The first Hebrew readers of Genesis, who lived in an agrarian society, would have understood all this to mean that the sun, moon, and stars were placed in the sky to serve the rest of creation. They told humanity when it was time to sleep, time to rise, time to sow seed, and time to harvest. Likewise, the plants depended on the sun and the rain for nutrients, and the animals depended on the plants for the same. We were created within a web of relationships with all of creation and with our Creator. And the text tells us all of these relationships were forcefully good.

Let's focus more closely on humanity's relationship with the rest of creation. Our relationships with the land, the sea, and sky were forcefully, vehemently good at a time when there was no such thing as fracking, oil pipelines, or mountaintop removal. The carbon count in the air was fine! There were no toxins to breathe in and no oil spills for ducks, seals, and fish to be mired in. The animals and plants had nothing to fear from humans because we cared for them. We understood that we too were created beings. Our misunderstanding of humanity's role in creation had not yet come to be. We did not think of ourselves as separate. We understood that we are creatures — not the Creator. As a result, our relationship with the rest of creation and God's order — God's reign and system of governance — was forcefully, vehemently good![33]

The writer of Genesis 1 reveals the nature of these relationships earlier in the text: "Then God said, 'Let us make mankind in our image [*tselem*], in our likeness, so that they may rule [*radah*] over the fish in the sea and the birds in the sky, over the livestock and all the wild animals, and over all the creatures that move along the ground' " (1:26).

Humans were made in the *tselem* of God. *Tselem* means "representative figure." This thought must have seemed revolutionary to its original readers. The Babylonian creation myth, called the Enûma Eliš, described a world where humans were created to serve the gods, who in turn were the embodiments of the various elements of creation, including the sun, the moon, the sea, and so on. Humans understood themselves to be subject to the whims of these elements, mere pawns in the games of the gods.[34]

But the writer of Genesis turns the Babylonian myth upside down, completely rejecting the notion that the pieces of creation are gods. In fact, to further distinguish the creatures from the Creator, the writer uses the name *Elohiym* for God, which means "supreme God." In Genesis 2:4 the author adds the word "LORD" (*Yehovah*), which means "self-existent" being. God is set apart from creation—God is supreme, the only one who is self-existent—not created, not one of the creatures.

And not only is all of creation subject to the supreme God, but the author of Genesis goes further. Humans are not, in fact, subservient to the elements of creation. Humans themselves are part of the rest of the creation, and what's more, all humanity is made in the image of God. Every human on earth— not only kings and queens, but also the widows, orphans, and immigrants—is worthy of the dignity, honor, and awe that the people used to reserve only for the social elite. To the writer of Genesis 1 this seems to be the most amazing part of the creation story, for even in the midst of explaining this point, the writer breaks into song!

> So God created mankind in his own image,
>> in the image of God he created them;
>> male and female he created them. (1:27)

The implications of this divine coup are tremendous. According to the Genesis 1 author, it is not the trees and rocks and sun that represent God on earth, but humanity. Humans are God's representative figures. Wherever we go we are markers of where the supreme self-existent God reigns. Every human being is endowed with inherent dignity because humanity is imprinted with God's own image.

But there is more: in the same breath, in the same sentence

in which the writer of Genesis 1 declares that we are made in the *tselem* of God, the writer says that God has given humanity rule (*radah*), or dominion, over the rest of creation. *Radah* literally means "to tread down"—but not to the point of obliteration. Poor biblical interpretations of *radah* have led to theological justifications for the exploitation of the earth. While it is true that humans are the pinnacle of the creation story and that humanity is given rule, historic Western interpretations of this Scripture have approached the text with the culturally laden assumption that *dominion* means "domination" and "exploitation." Twisted readings have even suggested that to exercise "dominion" meant that God ordained humanity to *improve* on the work of creation.[35] This was the justification for the establishment of land laws used to seize lands away from those who were not perceived as improving the land. As we will explore in more detail in chapter 2, which focuses on the genocide of indigenous peoples, the Native peoples of North and South America lost their legal claim to it.

This gross misinterpretation of Genesis 1 led Western civilization to place itself above and apart from the rest of creation and even above and apart from the rest of humanity. As a result, "civilized" humanity is neither creature nor Creator and has seized for itself unlimited authority to exploit both the land and "less civilized" humans for its own gain. The exploitation of the continent of Africa offers a salient example of the fruit of this mindset.

For nearly two hundred years governments established the trans-Atlantic slave trade to exploit Africa's human resources—people made in the image of God. These people were called chattel, and on all US census documents through 1860, they were classified as nonhuman property, legally considered no different than horses, buggies, or livestock. At the same time, enslaved Africans in the US were counted as three-fifths of a human being for tax purposes. This was done to determine the number of legislative representatives allotted to congressional districts in the South, thereby increasing the number of Southern representatives in Congress. In the twentieth and twenty-first centuries multinational corporations have extracted the African continent's rich mineral resources in an effort to maintain the affluent way of life of Western developed countries. Such exploitation has caused draught, famine, extreme poverty, government corruption, and triggered multiple genocides across Africa. Even some Western theologians created strong rationales for their own society's authority to rule, but with little accountability to the rest of humanity, to creation, or to God for its actions.

We argue instead that Hebrew agrarian society would have read the word *radah* to mean not "dominate" but something more akin to "steward," "to care for." It would have suggested our responsibility to maintain the boundaries of creation, to maintain its wellness. That would not have meant that wilderness would have to be left untouched. Rather, as Randy Woodley explains in *Shalom and the Community of Creation*, the biblical mandate to steward the land is codified into Jewish law for the people of Israel. In the Ten Commandments, God commands the people to honor the Sabbath. One of the mandates of the Sabbath is the call for all animals to rest every seven days. Then every seven years the people are commanded to enact a Sabbath year (Leviticus 25:1 – 7) — a year when even the land itself must rest.

John Steinbeck offers a devastating picture of the outcome of unrelenting exploitation of the soil in modern American history. His depiction of the 1930s Dust Bowl in *The Grapes of Wrath*, published in 1939, implicates the era's transition from family farms with diversified crop systems to bank-owned farms that were forced to mono-crop. Diversified crops provided the land's shallow top soil with periods of rest from its high demands for water and nutrients as crops with varying needs were planted and harvested at different times throughout the year. Mono-cropping offered no such rest. The Midwest's shallow top soil was continually subjected to unrelenting demands for water from a single high-demand crop throughout the year. The outcome was the Dust Bowl, a period of severe dust storms that nearly destroyed the ecology and agricultural capacity of much of the US.

As creatures made in the image of God, created to represent God on earth, we should mirror the kind of dominion over creation that God exercises. Genesis 1 paints a picture of that dominion. Again, the writer tells us that all of the relationships between the things God created are *forcefully* good at the end of the sixth day.

One key marker of God's dominion, therefore, is that it establishes and protects the wellness of all these relationships, including the relationship between humanity and God, humans with each other, and humanity with the rest of creation. If humans' dominion is to reflect God's, it must steward and protect the wellness of all the relationships declared "very good" after their creation.

God's dominion also provides for and serves the needs of all under his care. No one needs to be afraid under God's watch, not even of the sea monsters in the deep. Sea monsters were a source of great terror for the Hebrews, so how profound it would have seemed to the original Hebrew readers that God even declares the sea monsters "good" as part of creation. It is clear—under God's dominion there is no need to fear.

Genesis 2 paints an even more intimate picture of creation and offers an even clearer understanding of dominion. In that chapter, God's hands are in the dirt, forming humanity from the very dust of the earth. Humanity is clearly not separate from creation; we are made from it. Humanity is placed in a garden and given the responsibility to "till and keep" it (Genesis 2:15–16), or "work it and take care of it" (NIV). The Hebrew word for "till" is *abad*, which means "to serve." The Hebrew word for "keep" is *shamar*, which means "to protect."

You see? In contrast to the cultural interpretation imposed on the text by Western theologians, the text itself tells us that dominion looks like servanthood and protection. Rather than calling us to exploit the land, God called humanity to serve the needs of the rest of creation and to protect the integrity of the relationships God established in the beginning. The story of humanity turns in the span of one chapter and it all hinges on how the first humans interact with a tree—a part of God's creation.

In Genesis 2, God tells humanity not to eat of the Tree of the Knowledge of Good and Evil because it will lead to death. In Genesis 3, the man and woman choose their own way to wellness, wholeness, and peace. By eating the fruit of the tree they do indeed gain the knowledge of evil—but at the expense of not trusting God. Their relationship with God is broken, but it does not stop there. Because we were not created in isolation but rather in a web of relationships, when humanity broke relationship with God, one by one every relationship that God declared *tobe mehode*—forcefully good—was broken as well.

Among the broken lay the relationship between humanity and the rest of creation. The animals were cursed as a direct result of our sin (Genesis 3:14). For the first time in the story of creation we see an animal sniping at a human being (Genesis 3:15). Then, the land is cursed because of our sin (Genesis 3:17). The earth produced vegetation and fruit in Genesis 2:9. Now, for the first time, the ground will produce thorns and thistles, and humanity will have to beat the earth to eat and live (Genesis 3:17–19). "For the creation was subjected to frustration," Paul explains in Romans 8:20, "not by its own choice, but by the will of the one who subjected it."

Who subjected the earth to frustration? Some might say God did, since God laid down the curse. Others might say humanity did by not trusting God's command in the first place. In either case, the curse was the result of humanity's rebellion, and creation's subjection to frustration is the natural outcome for the land when the ones who were called to serve and protect it choose instead to serve and protect their own interests apart from God, at the expense of the rest of creation. As such, creation stands as a witness to the state of our relationship with God.

Theologian Paul Tillich said, "Sin is separation."[36] Genesis teaches us what the "good" is—yes, even the "forcefully good." It is simply right-relatedness. If the wellness of all the interconnected relationships in creation is good, then sin is, indeed, separation. Sin is anything that breaks any of the relationships that God declared forcefully, abundantly, vehemently good in Genesis 1.

As already mentioned, humanity continues to break the relationship between ourselves and the rest of creation. And so creation groans. Creation groans under the pain and frustration of trying to live out its purpose or producing the life-giving vegetation and oxygen that the animals need, including humanity,[37] and the animals groan trying to enrich the earth and produce enough carbon dioxide for plant life to breathe. All of creation groans under the weight of trying to reproduce vegetation at a sustainable rate while humanity is determined to secure its own wellness through increased deforestation.[38] Creation groans as agribusiness exploits the land through mono-cropping[39] and rapes the land through the increased use of genetically modified crops,[40] which in turn increases the need for ever stronger pesticides, which in their turn compromise the well-being of both human consumers and the land.

Creation is groaning under the frustration of trying

to reproduce natural gas and oil at a sustainable rate, while humanity is hell-bent on getting its energy fix right now, from every possible corner of the earth. The earth cannot sustain the level of carbon emissions created by our overconsumption, and as the seas warm and rise and as the climate is altered, both animals and humans—especially the poor—are at risk.[41]

And creation groans because humanity cannot avoid the repercussions of its addiction. Think BP oil spill. Think pipeline breaks in Utah, Arkansas, Nebraska, and Michigan. Think Fukushima and Three Mile Island. This is the definition of frustration and futility. We were created in the context of relationship with the rest of creation. We were charged with the responsibility to steward, serve, and protect our fellow creatures. Yet human exploitation of the land has led to its mounting destruction and a break in the stewardship relationship that God established.

And so creation is groaning for the revelation of the children of God. Its groaning serves as a sign of imperfect restoration now and the promise of perfect restoration to come. For we know the end of the story. The children of God will be revealed: Those who follow the Spirit of God will be revealed. Those who follow the ways of God will be revealed. Those who work for the reconciliation of all relationships broken at the fall—the relationship between humanity and God, as well as the relationship between humanity and the rest of creation—will be revealed. For who are the children of God? They are the ones who follow their father. And where is the reign of God alive and well? It is alive wherever there are those who obey and follow the ways of God. For, according to the Scripture, the revelation of God's children is a sign that the reign of God and full restoration is at hand.

Here is the question for the church today. Will we continue to argue over whether the earth was made in seven days or seven million years? Or will we *be* the children of God that we claim to be? Will we bear God's image and exercise God's kind of dominion? Will we humble ourselves and pray as God calls us to pray in 2 Chronicles 7:14? Will we seek God's face and let our Spirit groan with his spirit? Will we be reconciled to the rest of creation? Maybe then ... God will heal our land.

Signs of Hope and a Prayer of Confession and Lament

A few years ago a group of faith leaders from across New York City came together to consider how their congregations could partner with poorer congregations to help them get more green space and healthy food in their neighborhoods—while working to find ways of removing all the toxins that had been dumped in their neighborhoods. The faith leaders decided to meet quarterly, and each time they asked experts to come and talk about the issues that were most pressing at the time. After a few meetings, the group formed a Food Justice working group as well as a Toxic Dumping working group.

One of the churches that sent representatives to these meetings was Metro Hope Church, a small ninety-person, multi-ethnic church in the heart of East Harlem, one of the most toxic areas of the city. Surrounded by highways, with several bus depots and very little green space, East Harlem has one of the highest asthma rates in the country. Metro Hope wanted to know what they could do to be part of the solution. How could they make life better (and longer) for their neighbors?

They decided to plant a neighborhood vegetable garden. The project took a few months, and almost every hand in the church touched a hoe, a rake, or a handful of seeds in the planting process. Their small backyard garden now provides fresh, healthy food for struggling church members and people in the neighborhood, and in the process they've built partnerships with other neighborhood groups.

Along with their own project, Metro Hope joined the Faith Leaders for Environmental Justice at their Food, Faith, and Health Disparities Summit where they deliberated for two days about ways the faith community could help fix New York City's broken food system and make every neighborhood a healthy neighborhood. Metro Hope worked with scores of religious leaders to submit recommendations to the City of New York for how the city's food system could be incorporated into the city's plan for sustainability. Those recommendations were reviewed and integrated into the mayor's twenty-five-year plan for sustainability.

a prayer of confession: lament for creation

Oh, God. We see it. We see the lie we have believed.

We have believed the lie that you don't care about the trees.

You don't care about the leaves.

You don't care about the soil.

You don't care about the roots and the streams of living water that flow from root to root.

You don't care about the zebras and the tiger fish and the antelope.

You don't care about the Atlantic, the Pacific, or the Gulf of Mexico.

You don't know the names of fish or foul we've covered and smothered in the crudest kind of oil.

We have believed the lies, O Lord.

We are independent.

We are not part of creation.

We are gods over creation.
We are gods.
We have believed the lies. O Lord!
Salvation is only about us.
Never mind your Scripture. Never mind the cries that rise
*   from the holy text.*
Creation is groaning under the weight of our sin.
Creation is waiting for the children of God to be revealed.
We have believed the lies. O Lord.
Forgive us!
Forgive us for the ways we have heard the cries of creation ...
We have seen the melted icecaps.
We have seen the emaciated polar bears.
We have seen the brown haze over the cities.
We have flown over rivers and waterways that used to
*   carry crystal-clear water.*
Now slick green sludge floats in wastelands uninhabited by
*   anything ... because nothing can live there ... anymore.*
Forgive us!
We have seen the effects of our sin, God.
We have seen the high levels of cancer in our neighbors.
We have seen wars break out on the other side of the earth.
To fill our insatiable thirst for diamonds, gold, corn for car
*   fuel.*
Yet we have not even cared for the neighbors you called us
*   to love,*
The neighbors we know and the neighbors we'll never
*   know ...*
The ones on the other side of the city.
The ones on the other side of the tracks.
The ones on the other side of the world.
Forgive us!
We see it with our own eyes.

We have believed the lies. O Lord.
It's all gonna burn with the rest of it, we've said.
Can't worry about the polar bears right now.
Gotta put more gas in the car.
Creator God, forgive us.
Christ, Redeemer, forgive us.
Creator God, forgive us.
And redeem …

CHAPTER 2

sins against indigenous people

Historical Overview

It is difficult to review the history of Native American people in the United States—and their relationship to Christianity—without becoming either numb to the atrocities or completely overwhelmed by the decimation of millions of people. The story of Native people is nonetheless foundational to the birth, development, and propagation of the American republic. In 1492, just before Columbus encountered the "New World," Native American peoples possessed rich cultural heritages with great diversity, including more than 375 different languages.[1] Historians estimate that the Indians, as they were mistakenly called by European colonists, had a thriving population of around 50 million on both American continents, with roughly 5 million of those living in present-day US and Canada.[2] By 1800, as a result of wars with the colonists, the devastating effects of disease, and the intentional massacres of Native people, this population had been reduced to about 600,000 in North America.[3] Although not the only factor, Christianity and the propagation of its ideals by thousands of colonists had devastating effects upon the Native populations.

European colonists used religion as a means for controlling and subjugating Native American communities. Christians operated on the fundamental assumption that they had been given a divine mandate—an obligation—to dominate and exploit the natural world. This belief affected not only the wilderness and animal life, but the people who had been living among them. Historian Alan Taylor writes: "As a result, colonizers regarded as backward and impious any people, like the Indians, who left nature too little altered. By defaulting to their divine duty, such peoples forfeited their title to the earth. They could justly be conquered and dispossessed by Europeans who would exploit lands and animals to their fullest potential."[4] It was a form of religious imperialism. As the Native American populations were being devastated by the new diseases that had been introduced by Europeans themselves, Christian colonists initially viewed the high number of deaths as the effect of a divine intervention that was "sent by their God to punish Indians who resisted the conversion to Christianity."[5]

In addition, the colonists killed and wounded thousands of Native Americans during the brutal wars of the colonial period. In 1636 and 1637, the New England alliance of the Massachusetts Bay and Plymouth colonies along with their Native American allies (the Narragansett and Mohegan tribes) fought against the Pequot in a brutal war. As a result, New England Christians nearly annihilated the Pequot tribe, and those who survived were either integrated into other tribes or sold into slavery in Bermuda. Alfred Cave, in his book *The Pequot War*, asserts that Christian ethnocentrism, in addition to economic incentives, was the cause of the war. The settlers viewed the Pequot as "evil" and themselves as "good," and this struggle between good and evil could only be won with the complete destruction of the enemy. The Pequot were savages, according to the Puritans, a view that made it all the easier to justify their horrific treatment and oppression. Sadly, the example of the Puritans' destruction of the Pequots only marked the beginning of the gradual genocide of the Native American peoples in North America.

Even when not at war, the colonists demanded that Native Americans abandon their tribal traditions and assimilate European culture and religion. Colonists simply saw the processes of cultural assimilation and the conversion of Native populations to Christianity as a part of the same project.[6] At that time, many Christians believed that Native Americans had descended from the "ten lost tribes" of ancient Israel who had dispersed soon after Israel was sent into exile in Babylon, as recounted in the books of 2 Kings and 2 Chronicles. The return of Christ, Christians believed, could not occur until all the tribes of Israel had been converted to Christianity (Romans 11:11 – 36), so leading colonists placed special emphasis on the conversion of Native Americans.[7]

While ministry to the Indians was one of the main goals of many Puritan planters in Massachusetts, another significant motivation was to gain access to Indian land and expand Puritan financial wealth. Since Native communities practiced a land-based spirituality, which depended on the land both for sustenance and for upholding tribal religion, Natives were resistant to the Protestant idea that the land was an economic commodity and a primary route to the accumulation of wealth. As the Atlantic colonies grew in population, demands for Indian land increased and more conflict ensued. Other European settlers, motivated by the example of the Puritans in New England, also sought to accumulate wealth and access to resources by taking possession of the land.

By the 1640s, a solution to the so-called Indian Problem had been found. Under the leadership of Reverend John Eliot (who was the compiler of *The Bay Psalm Book,* the first book printed in the English colonies), Puritans established "Prayer Towns" throughout New England, which served the dual purpose of Christianizing the Native Americans while also removing them bodily from the coveted land. This allowed white colonists to seize possession of Native lands. Alan Taylor ominously describes the Prayer Towns this way: "Because the English could not conceive of permitting the Indians to remain independent and culturally autonomous peoples, they had to convert or die."[8]

Roman Catholics also adopted a model of Native abuse and subjugation. The Spanish established Catholic missions throughout Florida, New Mexico, and much of the North American south. Again, disease and physical abuse took brutal tolls on the indigenous population, who were subjected to forced conversion and abusive labor practices. Spanish missions served the purpose of not only propagating Christianity, but also consolidated Spanish control over the interior of North America much more cheaply and efficiently than soldiers would have been able to. The goal of the missions included the transformation of Indians into Spaniards (Hispanics) so that they would eventually compensate the Spanish crown by becoming taxpaying citizens.[9]

Farther north, Jesuit missions in the Huron villages of the Great Lakes led to almost complete eradication of the Huron tribe at the hands of these religious imperialists. Representing a common belief of the day, a Jesuit priest said: "Let them be killed, massacred, burnt, roasted, broiled, and eaten alive—patience! that matters not, so long as the Gospel takes its course, and God is known and souls saved."[10] Lest one thinks that this attitude was only endorsed by Catholics, a Protestant colonial minister expressed similar sentiments by insisting that "till their Priests and Ancients have their throats cut, there is no hope to bring them to conversion."[11]

While conversion was one goal, the quest for wealth characterized nearly all of the white settlers' encounters with Native Americans. The Puritan belief in predestination led them to focus on "good works" as a way of ensuring their election—their "chosen-ness"—for eternal life in the kingdom. Of course, people had no way of knowing whether they were among the elect, but good works served as an indication of God's favor. This was the root of the Protestant work ethic. But this same emphasis on good works often included the idea that the wealthy were similarly blessed and "chosen" by God. Wealth, therefore, was something to be pursued.[12] As colonists sought wealth and prosperity, conflicts with indigenous communities increased. Similarly, religious controversies with Native Americans grew more common, and "missionaries became one of the most vocal forces in demanding that tribal political activity be suppressed, since it was apparent to them that the religious and political forms of tribal life could not be separated."[13] Across the continent, Native American communities experienced harsh treatment, abuse, and war as a result of the Europeans' quest for power, territory, and financial gain.

As Christianity spread among the Native population, US government authorities outlawed tribal religions and forced many Native Americans into mission schools, which progressed following the Prayer Town movement of the seventeenth century. As mission projects, Christian boarding schools were then established to work directly with the government to help subdue and control the troublesome Native American people.

Supported by President Ulysses S. Grant's Peace Policy of 1869, missionaries targeted Native children in their efforts to Christianize the Indians. In time, Christian denominations became responsible for the administration of Native reservations, and the mission schools became more institutionalized, with many surviving to this day. The plan was "to separate children from their parents, inculcate Christianity and white cultural values, and encourage [force] them to assimilate into the dominant society through off-reservation schools."[14] The schools forbid the use of Native languages along with other distinct cultural expression and intentionally worked to "inculcate patriarchal norms into Native communities so that women would lose their place of leadership in Native communities."[15] In addition, sexual, physical, and emotional abuse was rampant within these boarding schools. In large part, the US government and the churches have not acknowledged the horrors of these abuses, though many survivors are now coming forward to tell their stories of medical experimentation, sexual assault, and other traumatic events.[16]

Even those Indian tribes that attempted to acculturate could not escape the powerful clutches of imperialism as the white citizens of the newly established United States continued to pursue opportunity for land ownership, wealth, and social mobility in the late eighteenth and early nineteenth centuries. After the 1803 Louisiana Purchase, the idea of Manifest Destiny became commonplace for most Americans, particularly Christians. It was the belief that God had specially ordained the United States to spread the values of white civilization from the Atlantic to the Pacific Oceans. Among the many consequences of Manifest Destiny were the complete removal of the five Indian nations, called "the Five Civilized Tribes," to Oklahoma; the conquest of Texas, New Mexico, California, and other parts of the southwest in the Mexican-American War; and the inclusion of the Oregon territory in the United States.[17] The story of the Trail of Tears of the Cherokee Nation, one the Five Civilized Tribes, is a powerful reminder of the devastating effects of greed and pursuit of wealth.

The Cherokee were among the most acculturated toward the ways of colonists along the Atlantic coast. Many Cherokee converted to Christianity and adapted to such white customs as the use of medicine, Christian wedding rituals, child rearing and inheritance, and the settlers' style of warfare.[18] During the first few decades of the nineteenth century, the Cherokee living in northern Georgia often assimilated by marrying white women, living in plantation-style houses, owning slaves, and operating large farms. Their children spoke English rather than Cherokee.[19] Even by British colonial standards, many of them were successful.

A single event in 1829, however, rendered the stable settlement of the Cherokee in Georgia precarious — the discovery of gold.[20] The hope of immediate wealth brought hoards of Georgians into Cherokee lands. Within months, President Andrew Jackson issued the Indian Removal Act of 1830, which would eventually force more than eight thousand Cherokees out of their homes to reservations west of the Mississippi River.[21]

One of the few Christians to intervene on behalf of the Cherokee was Congregationalist missionary Reverend Samuel Worcester. While other missionaries focused largely on the acculturation and Westernization of the Native people in addition to their conversion, the Congregationalists engaged the Cherokee primarily with the "purpose to acquaint the Indians with their God and Creator and what he had done and suffered to save them,"[22] In other words, their goal was to save souls, not to impose white men's ways.

While he lived among them, Reverend Worcester valued the Cherokee as people, understood their culture, obeyed their laws, and offered assistance even to the point of being imprisoned for fifteen months. When he attempted to intervene with the State of Georgia and the federal government on behalf of the Cherokee, in an attempt to allow them to remain on their ancestral lands, the Cherokee named him a "faithful friend to the tribe."

In the Supreme Court case *Worcester v. Georgia* (1832) Chief Justice John Marshall "gave the definitive statement on the status of Indian tribes under the Constitution," and identified Worcester as the representative of the Cherokee since they did not have legal authority to represent themselves.[23] Despite extreme sacrifice, harassment, and imprisonment, however, Worcester proved unsuccessful. According to historian John Ehle, "The missionaries to the Cherokees, in their efforts to play a political hand, had been defeated. They could preach in the other states, they could teach, but they could not influence political action in Georgia."[24]

And thus began the Trail of Tears, the forced removal of the Cherokee from Georgia to the Oklahoma territory. The Cherokee, along with a few other tribes, experienced extreme suffering and brutality for no other reason than the white man's pursuit of wealth. Over the next few years, tens of thousands of native peoples were forced to journey westward, and thousands lost their lives as a result of disease, malnutrition, and exposure.

But the discovery of gold in Georgia in 1829 was only a precursor to the massive population shift toward the frontier and the West after the discovery of gold in California in 1849. Vine Deloria Jr. writes of the effects: "The miners embarked on a program of systematic genocide against the Indians of California, and whole tribes were massacred to prevent them from holding their lands intact and out of reach of the gold-crazed miners."[25]

Across the country, as the result of land expansion and forced removal, Native Americans also suffered from prejudice, brutal treatment, and even massacre. There are even instances of white Christians massacring Native American Christians. For instance, the Gnadenhutten Massacre, also known as the Moravian Massacre, occurred on March 8, 1782, in Ohio. White colonial militia during the American Revolutionary War executed ninety-six Christian Lenape (Delaware) Indians who had spent the night before their execution in prayer and singing Christian hymns. A Lenape chief described his response to Christianity as a result of this horrific incident:

> They told us a great many things which they said were written in the Book; and wanted us to believe it. We would likely have done so, if we had seen them practice what they pretended to believe— and acting according to the good words which they told us. But no! While they held the big Book in one hand, in the other they held murderous weapons—guns and swords—wherewith to kill us poor Indians.[26]

More than half a century later, in 1864, Methodist minister John M. Chivington led another famous massacre at Sand Creek, Colorado, which killed more than a hundred men, women, and children and destroyed a village of friendly Cheyenne and Arapaho Indians. Reverend Chivington justified the massacre this way: "Damn any man who sympathizes with Indians!... I have come to kill Indians, and believe it is right and honorable to use any means under God's heaven to kill Indians."[27] Christians like Chivington often led the charge in pursuit of Western lands and material gain while brutally murdering Native American people.

Injustices toward Native communities continued well into the twentieth and even the twenty-first centuries. Native Americans still suffer from prejudice, lack of protection by the federal government, and exclusion from opportunities for social mobility within mainstream society.

A primary example of this exclusion is seen in the battles about whether nonwhite peoples can be buried in Christian cemeteries. In 1950, during the Korean War, Sergeant First Class John Raymond Rice, a Winnebago Indian, was killed in action while leading his squad in South Korea. After his body returned home, Christians in Sioux City interrupted his funeral and demanded that his body be taken away.[28] These Iowan Christians objected to the burial because they felt the cemetery should be reserved for whites only. Vine Deloria Jr. writes of the affair: "To the great embarrassment and grief of the family, the body remained unburied until finally accepted for burial in Arlington National Cemetery."[29]

Although many Americans were outraged, the incident was typical of how some Christians continued to exert racism, prejudice, and exclusionism toward the Native American community. Deloria continues, "One can only conclude that the Christian religion and its promise of the afterlife is not meant for nonwhites; Christians either do not believe in the resurrection, or they exclude nonwhites from their heaven."[30]

Even as blacks and other minorities gained legal protections, such as the right to vote and access to jobs, during the Civil Rights era in the US, many of the legal rights of Native Americans which had previously been assured by the government were being taken away. Longstanding agreements with the federal government regarding land use, game licenses, fishing rights, and tax enforcement were slowly being watered down or eliminated.[31] Native communities faced serious challenges in the areas of political sovereignty, economic development, constitutional reform, cultural and language maintenance and promotion, land and water rights, religious freedom, health and social welfare, and education. Today the Native American community is among those most devastated by drugs, alcohol abuse, domestic violence, and crime.[32]

Christians must confess the many ways we have contributed to this tragic history by acknowledging and repenting of our sins. We need to repent of our attitudes about the divine right of conquest, white supremacy, ethnic superiority, Manifest Destiny, the pursuit of wealth, and the brutalization, domination, and murder of thousands of Native people who have lived before us.

Theological Reflections

Blond locks float from the crown of Columbia, a popular eighteenth-century goddess figure that symbolized America. Columbia, which means "the land of Columbus," floats high above the frontier. She faces west. Sprawled before her is a dark and foreboding terrain, the Rocky Mountains, the wilderness. Driven westward, a bear looks upward at Columbia and roars, buffalo run into the darkness, and Native Americans on horseback and on foot flee into the dark oblivion.

Under Columbia's protection, frontiersmen walk westward in the distant company of a covered wagon and a stagecoach, while a man of European descent guides two oxen and digs his plow into fenced-in earth—shaping, grooming, cultivating. At Columbia's back lies the east; the source of the light. Three locomotives roar westward across the prairie, and in the distant east can be seen the Hudson River, the populated island of Manhattan, and the unfinished Brooklyn Bridge. Massive ships teem the harbor—all facing westward. Finally, in Columbia's left hand she holds telegraph wire, which she has strung across the continent from New York City to the plains. She looks west—determined, holding a school book, ready to pierce the darkness with progress.

This popular late-nineteenth-century painting by John Gast is called *American Progress*. Painted around 1872, it became the visual image of Manifest Destiny, which was itself one of the primary spiritual narratives that fueled westward expansion. The miners, the trappers, the frontiersmen, the women, the soldiers—all of them believed we had "God on our side."

By the mid-nineteenth century, mining companies and boomtowns were handing out pamphlets that featured Gast's divine Columbia, luring impoverished immigrants from the slough of eastern slums, across the Mississippi River, over the Rockies, through Death Valley, to the land where gold flows in the rivers of California. Droves of "pioneers," as we call them—though the land had already been well traversed for thousands of years by indigenous nations—left home and family to pursue their dreams and a nation's destiny under the unequivocal protection and justification of God. In their minds, God had ordained that they bring civilization—and therefore redemption—to this vast untamed wilderness.[33]

While we are familiar with the narrative, we are not half so familiar with its implications and outcomes: the military campaigns to exterminate and remove human beings from land that they had occupied for tens of thousands of years;

the diseases that Europeans brought with them that wiped out whole indigenous nations; the forced and coerced Christianization, which was actually a Europeanization of peoples whose indigenous stories often already gave them the profound potential to understand a biblical Creator God, God's son Jesus, and his purposes.[34]

The underlying assumption of the Manifest Destiny narrative is that God wants humanity to accumulate wealth;[35] that God's chief desire is for humanity to civilize creation; that humanity is separate from creation and can therefore be removed from it and exploit it without consequence; that human actions taken in the pursuit of "destiny" are justified no matter what; and, most profoundly, that humans become human and possess basic rights only *after* Christian conversion, which ultimately means conversion to Western cultural assumptions. But the consequences of these assumptions have been devastating.

The concept of Manifest Destiny was not born in the nineteenth century. It stemmed from the root of one of the earliest sermons ever preached on American soil, John Winthrop's "City Upon a Hill" (1630). In this oft quoted sermon, Winthrop, a wealthy governor of the Massachusetts Bay Colony (the second Pilgrim colony after Plymouth), drew from two key biblical narratives to frame the new American experience as a divine opportunity ordained by God; the narrative of the Acts community and the narrative of the Israelites entering Canaan — the land given to the Israelites by God. Winthrop called the colony to live according to these narratives in order to bring about two key outcomes: the global witness of the gospel and the possession of the land.[36]

First, Winthrop called on the new Americans, who arrived on the continent only thirty-eight years after Columbus, to embody an Acts 2 and 4 kind of community life:

> wee must be knitt together in this worke as one man, wee must
> entertaine each other in brotherly Affeccion, wee must be willing
> to abridge our selves of our superfluities, for the supply of others
> necessities, wee must uphold a familiar Commerce together in all
> meekenes, gentlenes, patience and liberallity, wee must delight in
> eache other, make others Condicions our owne rejoyce together,
> mourne together, labour, and suffer together, allwayes haveing
> before our eyes our Commission and Community in the worke,
> our Community as members of the same body, soe shall wee keepe
> the unitie of the spirit in the bond of peace,...[37]

Winthrop admonished the people to work as one community, to sacrifice economically for the good of all, and to exercise commerce for the commons. Thereby, he explained, their witness in the world would be magnified.

Then Winthrop transitioned into a comparison between the colonists and the Israelites who entered and took Canaan:

> And to shutt upp this discourse with that exhortacion of Moses
> that faithfull servant of the Lord in his last farewell to Israell Deut.
> 30. Beloved there is now sett before us life, and good, deathe and
> evill in that wee are Commaunded this day to love the Lord our
> God, and to love one another to walke in his wayes and to keepe
> his Commaundements and his Ordinance, and his lawes, and the
> Articles of our Covenant with him that wee may live and be multi-
> plyed, and that the Lord our God may blesse us in the land whether
> wee goe to possesse it.[38]

Casting the colonists in the role of protagonists in one of the most significant biblical narratives, Winthrop warned that, like the Israelites, if these English Pilgrims wanted to possess this land, they would have to abide by God's commandments and honor their covenant with God.

But his exhortations bring some questions to mind. For instance, what spiritual and biblical assumptions form the basis of Winthrop's Scriptural exegesis, and what choices spring from those assumptions? How did those assumptions affect his actions? And how did they help lay the foundation for the colonists' interactions with Native Americans in the era of Manifest Destiny?

Winthrop assumed that the Puritans had been called by God to this new world to possess the land just as the Israelites had been called to possess the land of Canaan. Like the Israelites in their exodus from Egypt, the Puritans had been persecuted. Like the Israelites, they sought a kind of freedom — religious freedom. Also like the Israelites, the Puritans encountered a land that was already inhabited. Yet despite these similarities, there is one glaring disparity: the narrative of the Israelites had already occurred, and Scripture gives no indication that God will repeat the work by setting apart another group of people on another special plot of land, at least not before the coming of the New Jerusalem in Revelation 21, which Winthrop does not reference. Also, there is no evidence in Scripture that God acts with any other group of people in the same way God acted with the Israelites. Thus, Winthrop's one-to-one correlation is, at best, flawed, and at worst, unbiblical.

Of course it is good to study Scripture for guidance in one's current context. But Winthrop makes a common, tragic mistake in his interpretation — he assumes that he is the "good guy" in the story. How different history would have been if the Puritans had cast the Pequot Nation in the role of the Israelites and cast themselves in the role of the Assyrian, the Babylonian, or the Roman Empire. Each of these empires invaded and possessed the land that God had given to the Israelites. In each case, the Israelites were massacred, removed from their own land, and sold into slavery, mirroring what happened to the Pequot Nation and most of the indigenous tribes in North and South America.

Finally, if we were to give Winthrop and the Puritans the benefit of the doubt and accept their assumption that their circumstances were exactly like those of the Israelites upon entering their promised land, a second question arises: Did the Puritans live up to the call of God in Deuteronomy 30? To answer that question, we must examine the commands of God that Winthrop references in his sermon — the Ten Commandments, which sit at the heart of God's charge to the Israelites. Three months after the Israelites' exodus from Egypt, God established his law among the people. Through the Ten Commandments God sought to consecrate these people (Exodus 19:10) and set them apart as "a kingdom of priests and a holy nation" (19:6).

What would this kind of holiness look like?

It would look like the first commandment: "You shall have no other gods besides me."

It would look like the second commandment: "You shall not make for yourself an idol . . ."

It would look like the sixth commandment: "You shall not kill."

It would look like the seventh commandment: "You shall not steal."

As mentioned earlier, the Puritans' desire for land and wealth was a key catalyst of the Pequot war.[39] With the great influx of settlers in the years that followed and the need for more land and wealth, the Prayer Town strategy was devised to remove the indigenous people from their land. Thus, the idol of wealth, which Jesus identified as a false God that sets itself up in competition with the priorities of God in Matthew 6:24 and Luke 16:13, is a driver behind the Puritans' impetus to kill people who were made in the image of God and to steal their land.[40]

So the answer is no, the European settlers did not obey the commands of God, nor did the millions of Europeans who came after them. Even by the Puritans' own Scriptural standard, God was obliged to judge their sin, not bless their wars.

The Pequot War was among the first wave of atrocities committed against the First Nations of this land. According to historian Francis Bremer, Winthrop sat on the council that decided to initiate the first battle in the massacre.[41]

We must face facts. Our nation's spiritual founders sinned. Their lust for land and wealth laid the foundation for the next two hundred years—with massacres, bribery, and theft of land. Our spiritual founders honored the demands of the idol, wealth, which Jesus characterized as the god Mammon, above the commands of the one true God, called both Elohiym (the supreme God) and Jehovah (the eternal and self-existent God) in Genesis chapters 1 and 2.

In a recent workshop where the authors of this book presented their findings, a young man referenced the second commandment's warning that the practice of idolatry will lead to judgment and punishment to the third and fourth generations of those who reject God. This young man asked, "When do we get to stop talking about all the things in our history? God says the punishment finishes after four generations. Shouldn't we be past this by now?"

Our answer was simple: "When we face and repent of the sin of the past and stop making the same sinful choices in present generations, then we can move on. Until then, with each generation we continue to mount judgment on our own heads."

A story in 2 Samuel offers a picture of true, deep national repentance. In the days of King David a famine struck the land for three years. When David asked God what had caused the famine, God answered: "It is on account of Saul and his blood-stained house; it is because he put the Gibeonites to death" (2 Samuel 21:1). The text explains that the Gibeonites were actually a remnant of the Amorites—one of the indigenous nations that was dispossessed of the land of Canaan when the Israelites entered it. In those days, the people of Israel had sworn not to wipe out the Amorites, but in his nationalist zeal King Saul had attempted a complete massacre of the Gibeonites. The text says Saul's sin against the Gibeonites is the reason for the judgment being made manifest through the famine during David's reign.

Consider this: David had nothing to do with the plight of the Gibeonites, and Saul's sin, while personal, had national implications because he was the leader of the nation of Israel.

How did David respond?

"The king summoned the Gibeonites and spoke to them.... 'What shall I do for you? How shall I make atonement so that you will bless the LORD's inheritance?'" (21:2, 3). This shows that David did two things: First, he entered into a dialogue with the ones who had been wronged, and second, he asked them what he should do to repair what was broken between them.

Lisa Sharon Harper once asked the late Dr. Richard Twiss (Lakota/Sioux): "How can we even begin to engage the sin against the First Nations of the Americas? Most people are too overwhelmed by the whole thing to even think about it. Let's face it. We're too afraid that if we ask what it will take to make things right between us, the answer will be: 'Go back where you came from.' So, people never ask."

Twiss answered: "Just be our friend. Come and talk to us. Get to know us. Get to know what makes us laugh and what makes us cry. And when you find out what we care about, then make our concerns your concerns. Make our struggles for justice your struggles for justice." That's what repentance looks like. That's what repair of what was broken requires.

And that is what David did. In response to David's questions, the Gibeonites answered, "We have no right to demand silver or gold from Saul or his family, nor do we have the right to put anyone in Israel to death." David presses again: "What do you want me to do for you?" They answered: "As for the man who destroyed us and plotted against us so that we have been decimated and have no place anywhere in Israel, let seven of his male descendants be given to us to be killed and their bodies exposed before the LORD at Gibeah of Saul—the LORD's chosen one." And the text says David's response was, "I will give them to you" (21:4–6). The text goes on to reveal that after the transaction was completed, "God answered prayer in behalf of the land" (21:14).

So what is the principle here? Should America start impaling people as a way of making things right with Native America? Of course not. The principle is this: The people who were wronged know better than anyone else what it will take to make things right. At the heart of Saul's sin, and Winthrop's, and the sin of every subsequent wave of domination over the indigenous peoples of the Americas was the sin of one people imposing their will over the will—and right to human dignity—of another, even as far as subjugation and death. Repentance is found in restoring the human dignity of the subjugated people. This happens in part by recognizing the God-given right of those who were subjugated to exercise dominion.

Genesis 1:26 connects the idea that humans are made in the image of God with God's command that they should exercise dominion (*radah*). As we've already seen, in its cultural context *radah* means "to steward"—that is, the ability to make choices and take actions that affect one's world. In turn, to diminish a people's ability to exercise dominion is to diminish their dignity as image-bearers of God.

Notice also that in Genesis 1:26 and 28 dominion is to be exercised over the earth and sea and birds of the air, not over other humans. It is not until after the fall, described in Genesis

3, that we see the first subjugation of humans by other humans. It begins with the subjugation of women under men in Genesis 3:16 and climaxes with the subjugation of nations under other nations, with kings and wars first mentioned in Genesis 14:1–16.

When David asked the Gibeonites "What do you want me to do for you?" he was restoring their ability to exercise dominion and, thus, their human dignity. By the same token, through submitting to the will of the oppressed, David recognized that his predecessor had attempted to usurp the role of God by determining who lives and who dies, who is worthy to exercise dominion and who is not. Even though David is the God-ordained king of Israel, he recognizes that his throne does not place him above God, nor does it make him more human than even the most marginalized in his society. He is as human as the Gibeonites. They, therefore, have the capacity to exercise dominion if given the opportunity. To exercise the kind of dominion that God exercises, then David will seek to serve and protect all. By submitting to the will of the Gibeonites, David forsakes the kind of dominion exercised at the fall and enacts a kind of dominion that is cast in God's image. In one step, relationship with both God and humanity is repaired.

One of the great political debates in modern American discourse is about the question of reparations. Are they necessary? Are they just? Are they biblical? Second Samuel 21 provides the answer to all three questions: yes, yes, and yes. Reparations are fundamental to repairing what was broken. Without active steps to repair, what was broken remains broken.

There are many ways to approach the question of reparations, but the fundamental principle is that it is not the place of the ones who sinned to decide how to repair the relationship. It is the place of the ones who have been sinned against to decide what repair requires.

Jesus became sin for our sake. His very body took the

lashings, the nails, the oppressive weight and humiliation of the cross. And hanging on the cross, sin is fully manifest as Jesus cries out, "My God, my God, why have you forsaken me?" (Mark 15:34). Sin is separation. On the cross Jesus is utterly separated from God the Father. When he breathed his last, he enacted the death that occurred in the relationships between the settlers and the First Nations, between every wave of immigrants and the original peoples who were forced onto the worst land and hidden from sight so that others could prosper. Jesus lived that death on the cross.

Jesus also offers us the hope of resurrection. In rising from the dead, he gave us hope for repair. He walked around in a body scarred by sin, and yet he lived. The resurrection of Jesus offers the people of the First Nations the hope of healing from the powers of death that have been visited upon them. The resurrection of Jesus offers the settlers and their children and great-great-grandchildren the hope of restoration to full humanity after stepping down from the false throne of divinity. And the resurrection offers us all the power we need to heal the relationship between the First Nations of this land and those who came after.

May we walk in the power of the cross and the resurrection. Amen.

Signs of Hope and a Prayer of Confession and Lament

At the InterVarsity Christian Fellowship Urbana Student Missions Conference in late December 2000, three indigenous leaders who are also evangelicals — Richard Twiss (Rosebud Lakota/Sioux), Terry LeBlanc (Mi'kmaq), and Ray Aldred (Swan River Cree) — sat down to share their stories. They were asked questions about their culture, faith, evangelism, and contextualization. They had a fresh message for the conference

attendees about InterVarsity's struggle to become a racially rec-
onciling movement. Soon other First Nation elders joined the
three, Randy Woodley, Brian Brightcloud, Cheryl Barnettson,
and Melanie McCoy. In the course of their conversations at the
conference the question of land use and protocol came up.

They explained that all cultures have protocols, ways of
doing things — good ways and bad ways alike. Indigenous cultures too have protocols, and some of their most significant protocols are connected to the use of land. The InterVarsity staff
adopted an attitude of humility and submitted to the teaching
of these elders whose ancestors inhabited this land thousands
of years before Europeans ever "discovered" it.

The elders called their attention to Acts 17:26 – 27: "From
one man [God] made all the nations, that they should inhabit
the whole earth; and he marked out their appointed times in
history and the boundaries of their lands. God did this so that
they would seek him and perhaps reach out for him and find
him, though he is not far from any one of us."

They explained that the Creator set the boundaries between
people as well as the ties between them. He determined the
lands in which they should live. The people are given spiritual
authority and responsibility to steward the land God gave them.
It is their responsibility to serve and protect the land, and it is
their responsibility if disharmony, imbalance, and sin brings
destruction to their land. This is true for all indigenous peoples
around the world, including North America — including
the land on which we live right now.

The First Peoples and Nations have been removed from
that land, and now the land is without the steward that God
appointed to protect and serve it. Instead, people came in and
claimed the land, built cities on it, cultivated it, and changed
it forever without regard for the spiritual authority of the First
Peoples of that land or for the well-being of the land itself. As a

result, the land is sick and the First Nations are sick. They have not been able to exercise their God-given command to steward the land. They are sick, and the land is sick because it lacks the spiritual covering and caretaker that God appointed for it.

From the beginning it has been the protocol that when one desires to travel through or to live in a particular land, one asks the leaders and elders of that nation for permission. This is done out of respect for the wisdom of the Creator who gave that nation authority over this place—and this is done out of respect for the land itself, out of a desire to do things in a way that maintains its wellness.

"Therefore," the elders told the InterVarsity attendees, "repentance for you would look like submission to the spiritual authority of the original peoples of the land even as you are deciding where you will live, where you will work, where you will plan your conferences. If one of the original sins was the sin of conquest and taking the land, then repentance will look like submission and humility."

The InterVarsity leaders took this to heart. One by one they began to practice this protocol as they planned for future national conferences, and some regional chapters began to practice the protocol within their regions. In every instance, they found that by recognizing the spiritual authority given to the First Nations of the land, the relationship with that nation begins to be rebuilt. Dignity was restored to the nation—and credibility was restored to the gospel.

a lament prayed in the voice, perspective, and experience of the native american community: psalm 12

Help, LORD, for no one is faithful anymore;
*   those who are loyal have vanished from the human race.*
Everyone lies to their neighbor;
*   they flatter with their lips*
*   but harbor deception in their hearts.*

May the LORD silence all flattering lips
*   and every boastful tongue—*
those who say,
*   "By our tongues we will prevail;*
*   our own lips will defend us—who is lord over us?"*

"Because the poor are plundered and the needy groan,
*   I will now arise," says the LORD.*
*   "I will protect them from those who malign them."*
And the words of the LORD are flawless,
*   like silver purified in a crucible,*
*   like gold refined seven times.*

You, LORD, will keep the needy safe
*   and will protect us forever from the wicked,*
who freely strut about
*   when what is vile is honored by the human race.*

sins against african americans and people of color

Historical Reflection

Even before the Pilgrims set foot on Plymouth Rock, African slaves were laboring on the banks of the Virginia Colony. In the nearly five centuries since then, racial injustice has marked American history, from slavery to segregation to lynching to discrimination, and throughout, the American church has all too often either maintained a disinterested silence or been the champions of racial oppression. The legacy of this history remains as a scourge on the story of Christianity in the United States.

One of Christian Europe's earliest rationales for slavery was that it provided the "heathen Africans" the opportunity to convert to Christianity. Slavery and its inevitable abuses, so it was thought, were a small price to pay when weighed against an eternity in heaven.[1] While many Christian denominations firmly believed in the evangelistic opportunities that slavery provided, many slave owners were concerned about the inherent leveling and equalizing impact of Christianity upon their slaves. Christian slave owners propagated the common belief that Africans were less than human and of another species altogether. The idea that black slaves were not created in the image of God eased the consciences of their Christian enslavers and justified their decision not to seek their conversion.[2]

While most Christians believed in the inherent value of the enslavement of Africans as a source for new converts for Jesus, many colonial planters feared that British law at that time would demand emancipation for any new Christians. The planters feared that slaves would submit to baptism for the sole purpose of gaining their freedom. To allay these fears, therefore, various colonial legislatures officially declared that conversion and baptism would *not* result in the freedom of slaves.[3]

Another obstacle for colonial Christians was simply the thought of having to share a common faith with African slaves. The biblical admonitions demanding charity, fellowship, and even a familial relationship within the church did not sit well with white slaveholders who depended on superiority and fear to control their human "property." For many colonists, faith was the core of their identity, and to blur the distinctions between Europeans and Africans on any plane could threaten their fragile racialized social order.

Virginia's colonial legislature even passed laws that served to increase animosity between whites and blacks as well as Native Americans. A 1670 law prevented baptized blacks and Native Americans from owning "Christian servants," although white Christians could own Christian slaves of color, further racializing slavery in the colony. This law only served to further equate Christianity with whiteness, as converts of color were never able to be fully included in the church. A decade later, the same assembly legislated a punishment of thirty lashes "if any negroe or other slave shall presume to lift up his hand in opposition against any christian."[4]

At the dawn of the eighteenth century, the Church of England made the strategic decision to reframe the relationship between colonial Christians and people of color, including Native Americans and African slaves. The church launched the Society for the Propagation of the Gospel in Foreign Parts to provide missionaries to the British colonies. These missionaries helped slaveholders undertake a moral duty to share Scripture and biblical faith with their slaves, and they suggested that Christianity would not unleash rebellion or promote equality, but would rather impose upon slaves a moral duty to submit, to work hard, and to be the most reliable and effective slaves they could be. These missionaries argued that slaves would respond better out of moral obligation than out of fear.[5]

This entire stream of thinking and praxis was rooted in the colonists' deep-seated belief in their religious and cultural superiority. As historian Albert Raboteau suggests, "With few exceptions, European and European-American Christians believed that they were justified in conquering American Indians and enslaving Africans to spread the religions and cultures of Europe, which they assumed were superior to those of other peoples. Church and state officials issued orders to colonists in America to arrange for the religious instruction of slaves."[6] This racial superiority became part of church culture in the American colonies and continued unabated after the Revolutionary War.

Following the Revolution, during which colonists had put their lives on the line for the principles of liberty and freedom, they had an opportunity to rethink the practice of slavery in the newly formed United States. Many northern states were on a path toward emancipating their slaves, but in the South the system had become too ingrained. The Founders knew the only way for the Southern colonies to join the new United States would be to allow them to continue to practice slavery. Even many white Christians who opposed slavery accepted a compromise to allow it to continue and ratified it into law in the United States Constitution in 1787. Tensions surrounding slavery did not disappear, however. The nation and the American church would continue to wrestle with this peculiar institution over the following eight decades.

To their credit, many early Baptist and Methodist preachers and circuit riders in the South denounced slavery. They sympathized with the abolitionist sentiments emerging in Pennsylvania and other Northern states in the early decades of the nineteenth century, but, as historian Christine Heyrman demonstrates in her book *Southern Cross*, much of the clergy in the south modified their views with an eye toward attracting plantation owners and slave masters, who were the men of consequence in the region. The clergy portrayed the church as being an institution of masculinity, violence, and white supremacy. Heyrman concludes, "Primed by decades of proving themselves men of honor in recognizably southern ways, Baptists and Methodists rose readily to defend slavery in the 1830s, secession in the 1850s, and the holy cause of upholding both with force of arms in 1861."[7]

As the debates grew more intense, the Christian Church in the South became more vociferous in its support for slavery, grounding it in white supremacy. Southern clergy began to offer biblical justifications for the institution. In 1857 George D. Armstrong, a Presbyterian pastor in Virginia, wrote a pamphlet called "The Christian Doctrine of Slavery." Armstrong argued that slavery is a consequence of sin, rooted in a curse upon Ham, one of the sons of Noah, the story of which is found in Genesis. According to the biblical narrative, Armstrong believed, after the great flood, Noah and his family planted a vineyard. When the grapes were ready, Noah made wine, became intoxicated, and fell asleep naked inside his tent. Noah's youngest son, Ham, saw his father's nakedness and, instead of covering him up, went outside to share the embarrassing situation with his older brothers. When Noah sobered up, he pronounced a curse upon Ham, saying he would be a slave to his brothers (Genesis 9:20–25). For Armstrong, this story of the perpetual enslavement of Ham and his descendants applied directly to Africans and African Americans.[8]

Armstrong was not alone. Christians around the nation and particularly in the South supported and reinforced racial stereotypes that buttressed slavery. Presbyterian James Lyon of Mississippi, for instance, suggested that the relationship between master and slave was "equal, in all respects, to that of parent and child," the only difference being that "a slave is a minor for life."[9] These sorts of pronouncements were not limited to a few clergy leaders. In 1864, as the Civil War was nearing the end, the general assembly of the Presbyterian Church in the Confederate States of America argued that "the long continued agitations of our adversaries have wrought within us a deeper conviction of the divine appointment of domestic servitude, and have led to a clearer comprehension of the duties we owe to the African race. We hesitate not to affirm that it is the peculiar mission of the Southern Church to conserve the institution of slavery, and to make it a blessing both to master and slave."[10]

Even after the Civil War, clergy like Benjamin M. Palmer, who served as pastor of the First Presbyterian Church in New Orleans for forty-five years (1857–1902), kept racist theology alive. Considered one of the pillars of post-bellum Southern

Christianity, Palmer replaced a vigilant defense of slavery with a strong call for segregation and white supremacy. He called for a racially separated church and society.[11] Palmer argued that when in contact with whites, African Americans "have never been stimulated to become a self-supporting people, under well regulated institutions and laws" and suggested the blacks regress into "their original state of degradation and imbecility."[12] This perspective was often the norm for clergy and congregants in the Southern church during the late nineteenth century, and enough Northern churches held to racist theology that the segregated church, buttressed by white racism, was the norm throughout the nation.

Palmer's views of former slaves harkened back to the days when colonists debated whether Africans had souls. He thought of blacks as young children, inclined toward disorder and rebellion. Thus, he believed slaves had benefitted from their situation as much as whites did, as slavery provided much-needed structure to their lives, and he wondered if former slaves would be able to survive, suggesting they could experience "rapid extermination before they had time to waste away through listlessness, filth and vice."[13]

But racist views lead to racist actions. For instance, during Reconstruction, the Louisiana state legislature in a progressive move prevailed upon the New Orleans Board of Education to admit black students in what had been all-white public schools. Rev. Palmer and the city's Presbyterians, in response, worked to establish an alternative private parochial school system that would cater to rigid segregationists by admitting only white students. One of Palmer's congregants led this effort. Not only did the church spout racist theology, these Christians also laid the structural groundwork for the codification of segregation.[14]

During the long periods of legally sanctioned injustice toward African Americans, from slavery and segregation to lynching and racial violence, perhaps the most damaging attribute of the church has been its deafening silence. James Cone, in his book *The Cross and the Lynching Tree*, focuses on the silence of the white church in the face of the lynching of thousands of blacks throughout the country. Of course, Christians were often more than silent bystanders. Cone notes that during "the 'lynching era,' between 1880 to 1940, white Christians lynched nearly five thousand black men and women in a manner with obvious echoes of the Roman crucifixion of Jesus. Yet these 'Christians' did not see the irony or contradiction in their actions."[15]

Most often, those clergy and Christians who did not participate in the lynchings failed to respond. Even so-called white liberal theologians did not pay much attention to the systematic terrorizing and murder of blacks through lynchings. Reinhold Niebuhr, the leading public theologian of the mid-twentieth century, spoke out against racism. But he also regularly advocated a slow and gradual approach to uprooting racism, even as the highly publicized murders of Willie McGee in 1951, Emmett Till in 1955, and "Mack" Parker in 1959 demonstrated the deadly cost of unchecked racism. Cone suggests Niebuhr's call for racial moderation "sounds like that of a southern moderate more concerned about not challenging the cultural traditions of the white South than achieving justice for black people."[16]

Cone's criticism of Niebuhr as a representative for white Christianity of the era reaches a poignant crescendo when he writes:

> Niebuhr could have heard of the nightmare in the black community from many people. While spectacle lynching was on the decline in the 1950s, there were many legal lynchings as state and federal governments used the criminal justice system to intimidate, terrorize, and murder blacks. Whites could kill blacks, knowing

that a jury of their peers would free them but would convict and execute any black who dared to challenge the white way of life. White juries, judges, and lawyers kept America "safe" from the threat of the black community. Thus, the nightmare in black life continued to deepen as progressive whites like Niebuhr remained silent about lynching.[17]

The consequences of white Christians remaining silent or unengaged on the issue of racial justice have always been severe, and far too many have paid the ultimate price.

Many point to the Civil Rights era as a period when the church was at its best. While this was true for many black congregations and a few progressive white churches, the overall record of the church during the Civil Rights movement is far from laudable.

A story from Montgomery, Alabama, in the early 1950s demonstrates the consequences of a silent and even complicit white church. One night, two Montgomery police officers arrested Gertrude Perkins for public intoxication. Typically, when a person is picked up for drunkenness, they are taken to the local jail, spend the night in a cell, and are released to relatives the next morning. In this case, however, the two officers took Perkins to a remote location where they sexually assaulted her. The officers were white; Perkins was black. Unfortunately, those in authority in the South and throughout the United States had often looked the other way when white males raped black females for over three hundred years. Nearly all of these stories are lost to history.

But this time, when Perkins was thrown out of the police car, she went directly to the home of Rev. Solomon Seay Sr., pastor of Mt. Zion AME Zion Church in Montgomery. Seay had the courage to send the story to a nationally syndicated columnist, who told Perkins's story to the entire nation. Other African American church leaders, goaded on by Seay, called for action and found an unlikely ally in Montgomery's own police chief, who called for the full prosecution of the accused officers. Montgomery's mayor and city commissioners did not support the police chief's efforts, however, and instead claimed the NAACP had fabricated the whole story. The offending officers' names were wiped from the public record, and no charges were ever filed.[18]

A few African American churches spoke out following the lack of action by the city, but none were as bold as the pastor of Dexter Avenue Baptist Church, Vernon Johns. As pastor of a congregation that sat a few hundred yards from the Alabama capital building, thousands of people saw Dexter's billboard each week announcing the upcoming sermon. Upon hearing that the city would take no action, Johns announced to all of Alabama the topic of his next sermon: "It Is Safe to Rape Negroes in Alabama." In contrast, there was no response from the white church in Montgomery following the rape of Perkins. They may have regretted the actions of the officers — but not enough to speak up or to be counted.[19]

The Montgomery community reacted quite differently to the arrest of Jeremiah Reeves. A white housewife had accused Reeves, an African American high school student from the Montgomery area, of rape and assault in the early 1950s. The word on the street was that the two had actually been having an affair, but when the woman's husband found them, she claimed rape and assault. Reeves was quickly arrested, convicted, and placed on death row. A few years later, on March 28, 1958, the state of Alabama executed Reeves for his offense.

On the day of his execution, Martin Luther King Jr. helped lead a prayer pilgrimage, attended by about two thousand people, to the Alabama State Capital building. When he addressed the crowd, King claimed the gathering represented "an act of public repentance for our community for committing a tragic and unsavory injustice." Although King claimed ignorance regarding Reeves's guilt or innocence, he questioned the unbalanced scales of justice, when "full grown white men committing comparable crimes against Negro girls are rare ever punished, and are never given the death penalty or even a life sentence." What was the response from the white church of Alabama to this prayer pilgrimage? They issued a harsh statement denouncing the gathering and paternalistically encouraged black clergy instead to sit down for dialogue with white leaders to work out their differences. When King and other black clergy asked for such a meeting, they never received a response.[20]

Unfortunately, this sort of behavior continued to remain the norm. From the Montgomery bus boycott right on through the Memphis sanitation workers' strike thirteen years later, the story of the white church remained uneven. Robert Graetz, who pastored a largely African American Lutheran church, was one of the few members of the white clergy to support the Montgomery bus boycott. A few white parishioners also encouraged the boycott, but most clergy and churchgoers were either silent or worse. Thousands who went to church on Sunday joined the overtly racist White Citizens Council (WCC) in early 1956, making the organization the largest in the entire county. Among those leading the church to the WCC was G. Stanley Frazier, the pastor of St. James Methodist Church, who joined the racist organization while claiming King and other clergy were attempting to "use the church as an instrument to destroy segregation."[21]

A few years before the boycott, the Southern Baptists of Montgomery had proudly built the Baptist Center, a locale for community ministry among the city's black Baptist population. When the boycott began, the Baptist Center became an ideal location for the newly formed boycott organization, the

Montgomery Improvement Association (MIA), to set up shop. This lasted less than two months. In late January 1956, the all-white board of the Baptist Center informed the MIA that it could no longer have offices there "due to the lengthy run of the movement and since it has taken on a political angle."[22]

Over the following decade of the Civil Rights movement, the initials *MIA* not only stood for the Montgomery Improvement Association but also for most of the white clergy throughout the nation who were quite literally MIA—"missing in action." Though some mainline white pastors did show up in Selma in 1965, their presence is notable primarily because it was so out of the ordinary. Most either remained quiet or even actively hostile during the long slow march to end segregation and to ensure voting rights for African Americans in the South.

In the meantime, some white clergy were continuing to work to offer theological underpinnings for white supremacy in the face of the Civil Rights movement. In 1965, conservative theologian Clifford E. McLain wrote a short book called *Place of Race*. The book offers biblical support for segregation by once again pointing to the sin of Noah's son Ham. Meanwhile, Baptist pastor Care Daniel wrote a sermon called "God, the Original Segregationist," suggesting Ham and his descendants, by which he meant those with African ancestry, were responsible for the destruction of Sodom and Gomorrah. Broadly implying a concern about the dangers of black sexuality, Daniel argued that "anyone familiar with the Biblical history of those cities during that period can readily understand why we here in the South are determined to maintain segregation." Daniel further argues that "the Bible clearly implies that the Negroes' black skin is the result of Ham's immorality at the time of his father Noah's drunkenness. For example, in Jeremiah 13:23 we read, 'Can the Ethiopian change his skin, or the leopard his spots?

Then may ye also do good, that are accustomed to do evil.' Here the black skin of the Negro is obviously a symbol of evil."[23]

Thankfully, racist readings of Scripture and theology like Daniel's have become increasingly marginal over the past several decades. Still, race continues to play a major role in American life. On nearly every quality-of-life measure, from poverty rates to education to health measures, blacks lag behind the rest of society. Most white Christians are not troubled by these statistics, chalking up all discrepancies to personal responsibility. As Michael Emerson notes in *Divided by Faith*, white evangelicals have great difficulty in seeing and responding to systemic injustices.[24]

A recent example of a crisis facing the African American community is mass incarceration. The prison population in the United States has grown from roughly 300,000 in 1980 to well over 2 million today, and the vast majority of these incarcerations are the result of nonviolent drug offenses. Even though studies show that the rate of drug use and trafficking is roughly the same in African American and Caucasian communities, it is actually young college-aged students who are most likely to use drugs. Still, the US government has chosen to wage their "war on drugs" primarily in communities of color, even though a more strategic location would be the nation's major universities. The results of this focus mean that some states have drug-offense incarceration rates that are anywhere from twenty to fifty times higher for blacks than for whites. The fact is that more black males are in the criminal justice system today than were enslaved in 1850.[25] Once again, until recently, the mass incarceration of people of color in the United States has gone largely unnoticed by white Christians.

Theological Reflection

In December 2013, one of the stars of the popular A&E reality show *Duck Dynasty* found himself in the middle of a national media controversy. The patriarch of the family featured on the show was taken to task for homophobic comments made during a magazine interview. Many in the evangelical community in the United States responded quickly, coming to the defense of the beleaguered television star. Somewhat lost amid the controversy were the comments made by the same *Duck Dynasty* star that indicated a severe misunderstanding of the racial history in the United States, particularly in the reality of sins enacted against the African American community. He claimed that African Americans in pre-Civil-Rights-era Louisiana were "singing and happy ... they were happy, no one was singing the blues."[26] In the rush to defend the star's right to free speech, many of his defenders failed to note his severe racial ignorance. The American Christian community easily misses such public expressions of racism.

Racism has deeply affected American society. We can observe its historical impact and its current reality in both covert and overt forms. That effect is usually seen in the realm of the material, but it is often missed in the realm of the spiritual and theological. Our best approach to understanding the systems of American racially based oppression is to view these systems as expressions of human sinfulness, expressions that are an affront to the holiness of God. As such, the church's historical contributions to slavery and oppression can only be seen as the deep blight of sin upon the church.

The sin of racism is best understood when God is the point of reference. As G. C. Berkouwer wrote, "Sin is only understandable in the glow of the fullness and majesty of God's activity."[27] Sin is the result when human beings attempt to take

God's place in creation and make themselves the standard for all decisions. Says John Stott, "To sin is, therefore, to take away from God what is his own, which means to steal from him and so to dishonor him."[28] Racism provides us with an example of the human attempt to elevate human standards in the place of God. Racism, therefore, is best understood in light of the doctrine of the image of God. In other words, racism is humanity's way of co-opting the image for its own elevation.

Every human being is made in the image of God, but racism asserts that the full expression of that image can only be found in certain races. Racism usurps God's right to declare what is good. The main expression of racism in the US is the theological distortion that elevates whiteness to a privileged position over other races—most evident in the elevation of whites over blacks. This distorts the doctrine of the image of God and links God's image primarily to whiteness.[29] Whiteness incorrectly becomes the embodiment of all that is good, true, and honorable. For example, during a news broadcast in 2013, a Fox News commentator claimed that both Santa Claus and Jesus were white. Underlying this comment is the assumption that a gracious, generous person could only be white.

The sin of pride undergirds racism. Pride is a misdirected self-love that regards others as being inferior to the individual or race. One of the objects of that self-love can be one's own physical appearance as embodied in one's racial identity. This sort of racial pride elevates whites to an almost godlike position and alienates people from one another. The white person's self-image becomes the norm by which other races are judged and measured. Whiteness becomes godliness.

The black person, therefore, becomes the opposite, and the question of the identity and worth of the respective races becomes a theological question. White superiority, and the relegation of blacks to the opposite end of the spectrum, is clearly a theological perversion. The story of Noah and his sons, therefore, is twisted to bolster white supremacy and does not arise from a correct understanding of the Christian Scriptures.

Scripture is often manipulated to confirm the assumption of white superiority. Theological interpretations of the created order are particularly susceptible to dysfunction. One approach to explaining racial differences, for example, asserts that the races were created separately and that different and unequal attributes existed from the moment of creation. This interpretation claims "that black people and white people ... belong to entirely different species."[30] Because black bodies had a different origin than white bodies, the image of God was attributed only to whites and denied to blacks. Since the Genesis account of creation is only applicable to whites, only whites can be considered as made in the image of God. Whites, therefore, had the authority to enslave blacks because blacks were not made in the image of God.

Another approach to white superiority arises from the idea that while all humans are descended from a common origin, racial differences arose at a later time. The story of Noah and Canaan in Genesis 9:20–28 provides the key source for this perspective. Noah's curse upon Canaan is interpreted as a curse upon blacks. While blacks and whites may have shared a common origin, God intervened to create a distinction between the value of white bodies over black bodies. Associating sin and evil with black flesh further established white superiority and black oppression. Of course, there is absolutely no connection between the curse of Canaan and skin color, and such a misinterpretation of Scripture was solely based upon the white assumption that black skin must be a punishment from God. This perspective fails to acknowledge the power of God's image in all humanity.

Both of these approaches reveal how the presumption that

non-whites were inferior led directly to a dysfunctional theological framework. A parallel example is found in the story of Louis Agassiz. A nineteenth-century Harvard professor, Agassiz was an American scientist who became a leading authority in the natural sciences. He perpetuated the belief that science supported the inferiority of non-whites. His analysis did not arise from any genuine scientific research, but simply from his negative feelings toward blacks. After first encountering African Americans Agassiz wrote in a letter to his mother, "It is impossible for me to repress the feeling that they are not of the same blood as us.... What unhappiness for the white race to have tied its existence so closely to that of the negroes in certain countries! God protect us from such contact!"[31] Agassiz' visceral racist "feelings" led to his racially biased conclusion that blacks were a different species than whites. Agassiz allowed his pride to warp science in the same way white Christians manipulated Scripture to construct a perverted theology based on biases and sinful thoughts.

Rather than confronting sinful racist attitudes, theology became the tool of an ongoing oppression. A warped understanding of the creation story and a warped application of the doctrine of the image of God becomes the justification for white supremacy. As Willie Jennings explains:

> Whiteness was being held up as an aspect of creation with embedded facilitating powers. Whiteness from the moment of discovery and consumption was a social and theological way of imagining, an imaginary that evolved into a method of understanding the world. It was a social imaginary in that it posited the existence of difference and collectivity for those in the Old World faced with the not easily explainable peoples and phenomena of the New World. It was a theological imaginary because whiteness suggested that one may enter a true moment of creation *gestalt*. Whiteness transcended all peoples because it was a means of seeing all peoples at the very moment it realized itself. Whiteness was a global vision of

Europeans and Africans but, more than that, a way of organizing bodies by proximity to and approximation of white bodies.[32]

White bodies, not God, became the norm of the creation account. The theological imagination could not envision a world with any other expression of humanity than white flesh. Any encounter with black flesh meant that the entire creation account had to be reimagined. Tragically, such theological reimagination was rooted in the assumption of white superiority and the elevation of white flesh over African.

Theories of white superiority were not limited to body and skin, but extended to the mind as well. The reimagining of Genesis yielded the assumption that white minds, and the products of those minds (such as language and culture), were superior to black minds and the products of those minds. The failure of the theological imagination again contributed to the warped idea of white superiority.

A notable example of the assumption of the superiority of the white mind is found in the primacy of European languages. John Willinsky reveals that "English is not taught as a *second* language but as the only medium of intelligible communication."[33] He observes that "to acquire the English language is to have a stake in its claim as a world language; it is to be a party to a history that runs from the colonial past that first planted English across the globe ... the linguistic chauvinism embodied in this notion of the native speaker sustains a colonizing division of the world."[34] In evangelical missions (as well as in the Christian academy), there is the assumption of English as the *lingua franca* of theological discourse. European languages in general are considered central to theological study, and the important works in evangelical theology are presumed to be written in English. English is considered a more important and central language for ministry. An Asian American pastor revealed that during a job interview in 2013, a denominational official mentioned that his knowledge of Mandarin could actually work against him in the candidate process. It was suggested that he only state his proficiency in English since that would improve his job prospects.

In addition to the use of language to elevate white minds over non-white minds, there is the elevation of white culture over non-white culture. Again, this cultural relativism is confirmed by a warped theological imagination. In an evangelical theology text titled *All God's Children and Blue Suede Shoes*, Ken Myers (as recently as 1989) makes the claim that there are gradations of culture in the world. He associates "high" culture (by implication a culture that is closer to God) with Western forms of cultures, such as Rembrandt, Bach, Greek philosophy, and then he contrasts "high" culture with "low" culture, which he equates with pop culture, represented by Bon Jovi, TV sitcoms, and Andy Warhol. Myers proceeds to create a third category that he labels "folk" culture, which describes such cultural expressions as Native American regalia, Korean drumming, and African dancing. There is a clear implication that classical Western culture holds a superior position to non-Western culture. Virginia Dominguez offers that "any positive reference to culture almost always implies a European and Eurocentric culture, which they claim as their own and in contrast to which they disparage others."[35]

Myers' bias toward Western white culture reveals the underlying assumption of the superiority of the white mind. Dominquez notes that this type of assumption "buys too unproblematically into an elite Eurocentric view of culture that would ignore issues of language, public rhetoric, immigration policy, education, class, race, and ethnicity that provide both support and challenges to that elite sense of culture as refinement and aesthetic achievement."[36] Additionally, Western

Christianity failed to see how other (non-Western) expressions of Christianity could actually contribute to their own theology. White culture was bound up with what it meant to be orthodox and what it meant to embody culturally acceptable Christianity. Christian identity, therefore, was tied to Western identity.

Warped theological assumptions about the creation account, God's image, anthropology, and human capacity (particularly as it relates to the value of non-white humanity) leads to a theological dysfunction when viewing soteriology. Not even this theologically essential topic escapes the dysfunctional theological imagination and oppression of white supremacy. Jennings captures this theological failure by revealing that

> white indicates high salvific viability, rooted in the signs of movement toward God (for example, cleanliness, intelligence, obedience, social hierarchy, and advancement in civilization). Europeans reconfigured Christian social space around white and black bodies. If existence between Christian and non-Christian, saved and lost, elect and reprobate was a fluid reality that could be grasped only by detecting the spiritual and material marks, then the racial scale aided this complex optical operation.[37]

How an individual moved toward God's salvation became linked to a physical capacity rooted in the white body, skin, and mind. Salvation was linked to the capacity to approximate whiteness, rather than the capacity to reflect God's image.

The link between proximity to whiteness and proximity to salvation is built upon the faulty theological assumption of white superiority in all matters of life, including physical appearance, intellectual capacity, linguistic ability, cultural sophistication, and spiritual possibility. All of these are predicated upon white assumptions of superiority, rooted in the unique endowment of God's image upon whites. Salvation for the African, therefore, becomes a process of moving toward an approximation of the white world.

Even the horrors of the slave trade have been interpreted as the movement toward whiteness and, therefore, toward salvation.[38] The African slaves were stripped of a central aspect of their identity when they were ripped from their ancestral lands. At the coastal "slave castles," they were separated from their families as another means of stripping away their identity. Transporting the slaves, first toward the coast, then across the sea, further removed Africans from their ancestral homes. The experience of the castle gate followed by their entombment in the slave ship reflected the death of the slaves to the life they once knew and the identity they once embodied. Salvation for African slaves was the process of dying to one's black identity and the transportation to the white world, the place of salvation as defined by white superiority.

The end goal of Christian theology is often cast as the pursuit of salvation. At times, the pursuit of that salvation is closely and intimately related to the death of Christ, even to the exclusion of Jesus' incarnation, life, and resurrection. With that backdrop, the slave trade experience paralleled Jesus' experience of death. In the same way that Jesus' Via Dolorosa aids the sinner in understanding Christ's crucifixion — the slave's forced travel experience became a way for the slave to experience Christ's death.

Willie Jennings discusses the parallel this way:

> Another crucial parallel between these two narratives is the central role of death. Christ takes on death to overcome it, while slaves are bound to death by being killed and through its use as a threat in order to subdue them. This is a reversal of the reversal, a christological deformation. That is, the body of Jesus will ultimately indicate the victory of God over death, but in this horrific scene the African's body indicates the ultimate victory of death.[39]

The centrality of death became the means of oppression for the African slave and the justification for slavery. The powerful doctrine of Jesus' suffering and death on the cross began to oppress rather than liberate. If the goal of the Christian life is salvation, and that salvation requires approximation to whiteness, then the non-white individual's experience of suffering becomes a part of the process by which whiteness is approximated. In other words, the suffering and death of blacks was a necessary aspect of the process of salvation for blacks. Slavery, then, could be justified since suffering and death are a means to salvation. As has been repeated throughout American mission history, the Christian can now find just reason for injustice as long as it leads an individual person to Christ.

The atrocity of slavery amplifies Christian complicity in the foundations of a demonic institution. The sin of the church is not only in its passive refusal to speak against the assumptions that drove the system of slavery, but also the formation of a warped and dysfunctional theology that ultimately provided the foundation for the slave trade. The church is guilty of both the sin of omission and the sin of commission.

Willie Jennings summarizes the dysfunctional theological imagination by stating that

> Europeans established a new organizing reality for identities, themselves.... Europeans enacted racial agency as a theologically articulated way of understanding their bodies in relation to new spaces and new peoples and to their new power over those spaces and peoples. Before this agency would yield "idea of race," "the scientific concept of race," the "social principle of race," or even a fully formed "racial optic" on the world, it was a theological form—an inverted, distorted vision of creation that reduced theological anthropology to commodified bodies. In this inversion, whiteness replaced the earth as the signifier of identities.[40]

A dysfunctional theological imagination leads to the elevation of white over black and, subsequently, the injustice of slavery now finds a theological justification.

Signs of Hope and a Prayer
of Confession and Lament

In April 2001, an unarmed African American teenager named Timothy Thomas was shot and killed by Cincinnati Police. Thomas's death was just the latest in a series of questionable deaths of unarmed African Americans by city law enforcement, and for a few brief days, the city's racial tensions erupted into uprisings and rioting.

At the time, Chris Beard was pastor at First Christian Assembly of God, a historic Pentecostal congregation in the heart of Cincinnati. Of the over five hundred attendees each Sunday, roughly 98 percent were white. The congregation did not reflect the demographics or the experiences of First Christian's neighborhood. Beard's first response was to repent of a history of blissful ignorance and lack of deep concern for those who lived in the same neighborhood as First Christian.

In the aftermath of Timothy Thomas's death, Pastor Beard made a commitment to transform his congregation into a church that looked more like its neighborhood and a church that looked more like heaven, rooted in the heavenly vision of Revelation 7:9: "After this I looked, and there before me was a great multitude that no one could count, from every nation, tribe, people and language, standing before the throne and before the Lamb."

Since 2001, First Christian Assembly has lived into Pastor Beard's vision. The congregation is now 25 percent African American and 25 percent international and other ethnicities. And the church is speaking out for racial justice, advocating for the voting rights of blacks in Cincinnati, and working to dismantle the devastating effects of the war on drugs and mass incarceration.

One of the more amazing stories of transformation at the

congregation now known as Peoples Church involves Terry Thomas, Timothy's younger brother. Terry was sixteen when his older brother was shot in 2001. Terry is now a member of Peoples Church, a growing follower of Jesus, and a loving father and husband, and Peoples Church is a congregation whose transformation is rooted in a spirit of humility, repentance, and transformation.

Think of the following lament as being spoken *not* from the perspective of our dominant white culture, but from the voice, perspective, and experience of the African American community.

psalm 79

O God, the nations have invaded your inheritance;
  they have defiled your holy temple,
  they have reduced Jerusalem to rubble.
They have left the dead bodies of your servants
  as food for the birds of the sky,
  the flesh of your own people for the animals of the wild.

They have poured out blood like water
  all around Jerusalem,
  and there is no one to bury the dead.
We are objects of contempt to our neighbors,
  of scorn and derision to those around us.

How long, LORD? Will you be angry forever?
  How long will your jealousy burn like fire?
Pour out your wrath on the nations
  that do not acknowledge you,
on the kingdoms
  that do not call on your name;

for they have devoured Jacob
and devastated his homeland.

Do not hold against us the sins of past generations;
may your mercy come quickly to meet us,
for we are in desperate need.
Help us, God our Savior,
for the glory of your name;
deliver us and forgive our sins
for your name's sake.
Why should the nations say,
"Where is their God?"

Before our eyes, make known among the nations
that you avenge the outpoured blood of your servants.
May the groans of the prisoners come before you;
with your strong arm preserve those condemned to die.
Pay back into the laps of our neighbors seven times
the contempt they have hurled at you, Lord.
Then we your people, the sheep of your pasture,
will praise you forever;
from generation to generation
we will proclaim your praise.

CHAPTER 4

sins against
women

Historical Reflection

In the fall of 1992, the state of Iowa prepared to vote for a state-wide equal rights amendment to guarantee equal rights for both men and women. During the summer, as coalitions for and against the amendment mobilized, televangelist Pat Robertson wrote a fund-raising letter through the Christian Coalition to work against the amendment and its feminist supporters. Robertson claimed the proposed amendment was "about a socialist, anti-family political movement that encourages women to leave their husbands, kill their children, practice witchcraft, destroy capitalism and become lesbians."[1] Although this is an extreme example, again and again for over four centuries, the church in the United States has used rhetoric and politics to work against the rights and dignity of women.

Of course, the United States is not alone. Throughout history, women have rarely experienced anything close to equality. Early in the book of Genesis, when God confronted Adam after he and Eve ate from the forbidden tree, Adam's first response was to blame Eve. In the gospel of John, the author includes the story of a woman who was caught in the act of adultery. When the "teachers of the law and the Pharisees" (8:3) — all men — brought the woman to Jesus, asking him what they should do to her, Jesus famously responded by encouraging those without sin to cast the first stone. Slowly the people left. But of course the entire story prompts us to ask, "Why didn't they bring the man who was caught in adultery as well?"

This uneven and unjust vilification of women in the Bible has also been part of American history since colonial days. Not only has the church failed to defend the rights of women in the public square, but it has also often participated — or even led the charge — in perpetrating injustice. These wrongs need to be confessed, and a pathway toward true repentance must be embarked upon to begin to atone for centuries of sexism.

One of the earliest and most sensationalized events in colonial history has a strong undercurrent of sexism. The Salem Witch Trials, which plagued that small town in the Massachusetts Bay Colony in 1692, were a symptom of the repression of women. Although the trials in Salem are infamous, they occurred at a time when witch trials were common, both in England (a fact that did not escape the attention of Monty Python) and in the English colonies. During this period, Puritans often suspected and accused women of having fellowship, conversation, and intimacy with Satan. In the years between 1630 and 1700, 234 individuals were indicted by a court of witchcraft in the Massachusetts Bay Colony, resulting in the executions of thirty-six suspected witches.[2]

The social mores of Puritan society, which rigidly controlled the public lives of females, helps explain the frenzy of those young women who accused so many other women of witchcraft. In a world in which the opinions and observations of young women especially were rarely noticed, these young girls commanded considerable attention when they accused others of witchcraft. They were invited to speak publicly, and their words had power to shape the fate of others. While other motivations for making such accusations were undoubtedly at play, the fact that they achieved some rare attention in the public sphere was at least part of the story.[3]

Although some of the victims of the Salem Witch Trials were men, the overwhelming majority were women. Demographic studies show that those most likely to be accused of witchcraft were indigent women between the ages of fifty and seventy, who frequently begged from their neighbors and cursed or grumbled when they did not receive charity.[4] In New England, many of those accused were not only the poor but also those who were financially independent of men. Historian Carol Karlsen claims that independent women caused so much anxiety that the accusation of witchcraft provided their communities relief from the threat of autonomous women. In the Puritan mind, any act that contradicted biblical commands was of the devil, and witchcraft became one manifestation of this evil.[5]

In Salem alone, a group primarily consisting of younger women accused 185 people of being witches. Of the 59 who went to trial, 31 were found guilty, and of this number, 19 were put to death, including 14 women. During the century when allegations of witchcraft were most common (1620–1725), 80 percent of the people accused, convicted, and put to death for associating with Satan were women.[6]

The church not only sanctioned the deaths of people created in God's image, it often led the crusade. While witch trials would fade into history, these tragic deaths where a grim precursor of how the church would continue negatively to engage women in the public square for the next four centuries in North America.

A century later, the life of Sojourner Truth demonstrates the continued complicity of the church with sexism and even misogyny. Before changing her name in 1843, Truth was known by her birth name of Isabella. She grew up as a slave in upstate New York, spending several years as the property of John and Sally Dumont, parishioners of the local Dutch Reformed Church. Not only did Isabella experience physical abuse at the hands of her owners, but sexual abuse as well, all from those who claimed to be followers of Jesus.[7]

After gaining her freedom around the time all older slaves were emancipated in New York State, Isabella changed her name to Sojourner Truth and became a familiar speaker at abolitionist, temperance, and women's rights gatherings in the North.

During a famous speech in Akron in 1851, Truth challenged the biblical defense of sexism rooted in Eve's disobedience in Genesis. She argued that if a woman had set the world off course by eating from the Tree of the Knowledge of Good and Evil, then women should be involved in setting the world to rights. Noting the pivotal role Mary and Martha played in Jesus' decision to raise Lazarus from the dead in the gospel of John, Truth insisted that Jesus is particularly responsive to the requests and prayers of women. After all, Truth claimed, Jesus came to earth through a union of God and a woman, with no involvement of a man whatsoever.[8]

Truth's bold advocacy of the rights of women elicited strong criticisms. Many were unwilling to accept a legitimate public role for women, let alone an African American woman who had formerly been a slave. When she spoke publically, mobs frequently gathered to protest, and on one occasion their hateful rhetoric led to violence. She was assaulted and sustained a permanent injury, which forced her to walk with a cane the rest of her life.[9]

Another incident, at an abolitionist gathering in Indiana, demonstrates how toxic the environment could be for women speakers. After Truth's speech, a gathering of pro-slavery men, led by T. W. Strain, argued that she was not actually a woman but a man. They took a vote among the congregation, and the majority concurred with the belief that she was in fact a man. The crowd, which undoubtedly included many regular churchgoers, went so far as to demand that Truth show her breasts to validate her gender. Truth obliged her audience but chastised them, saying that "it was not to her shame that she uncovered her breast before them, but to their shame."[10]

Following the Civil War, women like Sojourner Truth began to focus on suffrage for former slaves and women. While the fifteenth amendment theoretically guaranteed a black male's right to vote (after reconstruction this right was slowly taken away), the struggle for women's suffrage continued for many decades. Not until 1920, more than fifty years after the Civil War, was the guarantee of women's suffrage finally added as the nineteenth amendment to the US Constitution.

Although many leaders of the suffrage movement were Christians, much of the opposition was fueled by the church's understanding of a woman's role in the home and society. Using rhetoric that would still be used by Pat Robertson a century later, many Christians accused suffragists of trying to undermine marriage, the family, and even the church.[11] In the minds of many, a woman belonged in the home, as a dutiful wife, nurturing mother, and suitable homemaker. Elizabeth Cady Stanton, one of the conveners of the famed Seneca Falls women's rights convention of 1848, famously asked, "What has

Christianity done for women?" For Stanton, the answer was obvious: precious little.[12]

To be fair, strong Christian leaders and congregations drove many of the reform movements of the nineteenth century, including abolition, temperance, and the call for women's suffrage. They grounded these movements on strong biblical and theological underpinnings. Frances Willard, longtime leader of the Women's Christian Temperance Union, claimed her work for women's suffrage was rooted in the prompting of the Holy Spirit.[13] Still, at least in the case of abolition and women's rights, many Christians and church leaders consistently participated in systematic opposition to any expanded role for women in the public sphere. So while an honest answer to Stanton's question "What has Christianity done for women?" would be more complicated than she suggested, her concern about the church's obstruction still has much merit.

During the late nineteenth century, debates over the role of women were rampant. Some conservative and evangelical Bible scholars, preachers, and theologians suggested that Paul's call for women to remain silent in church should be extended to the public arena as a whole. A woman's rightful place for speech and teaching, they felt, was in the private sphere, the home, particularly as mothers. One biblical commentary of the day went so far as to interpret 1 Corinthians 14:34, "Let your women keep silence in the churches," to mean the entire public realm: "In your congregations, as in all congregations of Christ's people, the women must keep silence; for they are not permitted to speak in public."[14] While debates raged regarding the appropriate roles of women in a local congregation or church, moving this restriction to the point of denying women all legitimate right to speak in public was a major claim that many began to embrace during the rise of the suffrage movement.

Some American religious leaders felt they were under assault at the dawn of the twentieth century, which may account for their extreme reactions to the call for women's rights. Historical criticism of the Bible, Darwinism, religious pluralism, and waves of new immigrants all seemed to threaten the hegemony of the Protestant church. As women pushed for a greater role in society and at the ballot box, they often explored new scientific theories and rationalistic approaches coming from Europe. Some women entertained the Free Thought movement, which elevated science, reason, and logic above faith, religion, and biblical authority. In response to those who attended Free Thought lectures, one of the leading Presbyterian orators of the late nineteenth century, Rev. Thomas DeWitt Talmage, argued, "If after all that Christ and Christianity have done for a woman, she can go and hear such assaults, she is an awful creature and you had better not come near such a reeking lepress. She needs to be washed, and for three weeks to be soaked in carbonic acid, and for a whole year fumigated, before she is fit for decent society."[15] While Talmage's concern for Christian orthodoxy warranted suspicion toward any who were seriously exploring the Free Thought movement, his hyperbolic response reveals the misogynistic tenor that often marked evangelicals as the century came to a close.

Talmage was not alone in his concern about the increased clamor for women's rights. Fellow pastor W. W. Patton, in a sermon called "Women and Skepticism," asserted that "the enlargement of woman's sphere tended to immorality; that women are governed by their emotions and are incapable as advisors in a world of action."[16] In Atlanta, during the convention of the National American Woman's Suffrage Association in 1895, a local pastor strongly critiqued all suffragists and their husbands as working against God's intended order.[17]

In 1920, near the end of the struggle to ratify the Nineteenth Amendment to the Constitution, which granted women the right to vote, Tennessee's legislature took up the issue, knowing that if they ratified the amendment, it would then become part of the Constitution. In response, anti-suffrage leaders pointed to controversial quotes from Elizabeth Cady Stanton's *Women's Bible* to brand the suffragist movement heretical. Many Christians worked tirelessly to defeat the amendment and solicited assistance in their crusade from "everyone who believes that the word of God is divinely inspired, who desires to his State Constitution not violated, and who believes in the purity of the family and the sanctity of marriage and would keep women out of politics."[18] According to Abbey Crawford Milton, a suffragist from Nashville, dozens of Christian ministers were won over to the anti-suffrage movement when they read the commentary in the *Women's Bible.* Since much of the commentary in Stanton's *Women's Bible* is anything but orthodox, those working to defeat the right for women to vote were almost successful by conflating theological concerns with human rights.[19] The anti-suffrage forces nearly won the day, in part due to the resistance of leading Christians, although in the end Tennessee ratified the amendment by a single vote.

The passage of the Nineteenth Amendment, however, did not end the struggle for women's rights. For the next several decades, attention turned to equal pay for equal work and fair opportunities in employment and education. Emblematic of this struggle was the attempt to add an Equal Rights Amendment (ERA) to the Constitution to ensure equal rights for women under the law.

While the basic premise of the ERA had gained support from both political parties as early as the 1940s, it did not take long for opposition to emerge. Conservative women like Cecilia Yawman of the Rochester Diocesan Council of Catholic Women urged her congressman to oppose the ERA for its inherent dangers, including confusing "equal rights with identical rights."[20] When the feminist movement began to gain traction in the mid-1960s, a real push for passing such an amendment emerged.

In 1971, by a vote of 354 to 23, the US House of Representatives passed the ERA and the next year the Senate followed suit, by a margin of 84 to 8. The proposed amendment was concise and to the point: "Equality of rights under the law shall not be denied or abridged by the United States or by any State on account of sex." The Constitution gives states seven years to ratify proposed amendments, and the ERA was passed in thirty of the thirty-eight necessary states within the first year.[21]

Soon after the ERA went to the states for ratification, however, the Supreme Court issued its landmark *Roe v. Wade* decision, which said that the Constitution's right to privacy extends to a woman's right to have an abortion. This decision, coupled with a progressive agenda from the National Organization of Women (NOW), led many Christians to take up the battle against the ERA in an attempt to win hearts and minds to stand against what they considered a radical feminist agenda.

Many Christians saw the ERA as emblematic of a society in which traditional cultural values such as family and childrearing were under attack. Popular conservative Phyllis Schlafly, a Roman Catholic, led the charge, arguing for the need to preserve the "Christian tradition of chivalry," which gives men the responsibility of protecting women. In Schlafly's view, the ERA represented a radical feminist agenda that was "anti-family, anti-children, and pro-abortion." She went so far as to assert that "women libbers view the home as a prison and the wife and mother as a slave."[22]

Schlafly became a leading spokesperson for the "STOP ERA" movement, an effort largely driven by Catholic and evangelical Christian women. A study revealed that an incredible 98 percent of those working to oppose the ERA identified themselves as church members, while less than 50 percent of those working for ratification of the ERA claimed church membership.[23] What emerged over the rest of the 1970s was a Christian-motivated fight to prevent the ERA from being ratified by associating the proposed amendment with abortion rights, gay rights, and the breakdown of the traditional family and culture.

Certainly some of the ERA's most passionate proponents were thrilled with the *Roe v. Wade* decision and argued for a progressive transformation of gender roles in American life. The argument about the breakdown of traditional roles and morality made by Schlafly and other Christian leaders of the STOP ERA effort was based on an honest assessment of cultural trends and heartfelt fears about the future of the nation.

Unfortunately, this largely Christian opposition to the ERA fit the repressive interpretation many women held because they had seen the church adopt an anti-woman and even misogynistic posture all too often throughout history. During the last three decades of the twentieth century, beginning with their passionate opposition to the ERA, the evangelical church in the US was identified as anti-feminist and even anti-woman. Internal church arguments about the use of inclusive pronouns rather than masculine pronouns in Bible translations and the controversy over the ordination of women only added to the church's anti-woman image in the culture at large.

Driven by fear, many in the church opposed a concise pro-woman amendment to the Constitution, but no matter how justified they believed they were, the result is yet another chapter in the history of the church that needs to be confessed. While many evangelicals had legitimate concerns about legally sanctioned abortion, the leap to a crusade against women's rights perpetuated a script that had been acted out far too often in

American history: Christians organizing to marginalize women in the public sphere.[24]

Another important trend to acknowledge is the church's deafening silence on the issue of domestic abuse. According to a 2013 US Justice Department report, 25 percent of women in the US have been victims of domestic violence.[25] Though this problem is not new, the church has, by and large, failed to show concern or raise awareness about the epidemic. It wasn't until 1981 that the more liberal National Council of Churches established a day of solidarity for victims of domestic abuse, and in 1987 they launched a Domestic Violence Awareness Month, to take place every October.[26]

More recently, some evangelicals have recognized the need to break their silence on the issue. In their recent book, *A Cry for Justice*, authors Jeff Crippen and Anna Wood call the church to become much more responsive to the reality of domestic abuse, noting that "the local church is one of the favorite hiding places of the abusive person. Conservative, Bible-believing religion is his frequent choice of facade. Within the evangelical church, women (and sometimes men) are being terribly abused in their homes and marriages. The children of such abusers are suffering as well."[27] The authors acknowledge that the victims, if and when they muster the courage to confide in a member of the clergy, are too often dismissed or are not offered the support they need to get out of destructive situations. At times they are even blamed for their abuse.[28] The church's inability to address this blight adds to a history that has often blamed or dismissed women and their challenges.

In 2003, Dan Brown's runaway bestseller *The Da Vinci Code* prompted outrage and protests from many evangelical Christians who were justly concerned about the conspiracy-theory-driven plot based on scant historical evidence. One of the reasons the book resonated so deeply, however, was because one of its primary themes rang true: the Church has had an anti-woman agenda for centuries. Unfortunately, thanks to quotes like that of Pat Robertson and centuries of actions and rhetoric that were at times anti-woman, the church needs to confess and repent.

Theological Reflection

Evangelical engagement on gender issues often responds to changes in the culture. In recent years, the notable level of tension around gender issues among evangelicals arises from a concern over changing norms and values in larger American society. A positive expression of this concern has been the increased awareness of social realities by evangelicals. The negative expression has been the revelation of deep-seated sexism within the evangelical community as well as in all sectors of American society.

Unfortunately, harsh lines in evangelicalism have been drawn that push individuals toward one perspective over the other with no room for compromise. The arguments have been heated and often lack grace. Rather than rehashing the familiar ground of the conflict between different ecclesial and denominational positions, this section focuses on the sins committed by the Christian community, regardless of one's particular perspective on gender roles.

For example, the issue of the ordination of women is not addressed in this chapter. But instead, we acknowledge the larger value of the doctrine of the *imago Dei* and the worth afforded to every human being by the Scriptures. We can then proceed from that central doctrine to examine the impact on the individual who is demeaned by sins committed against women. We will also examine the theological implications and sociological impact of the church's corporate sins against women and its harmful effects on our Christian witness to the world.

Our understanding of Scripture should form the foundation of our engagement on the topic of gender. As with other issues discussed in this book, current conversations on gender would benefit from a deeper understanding of the key doctrine of the *imago Dei*. Understanding this doctrine would place the emphasis on God's pronouncement over human identity rather than relying upon derivative understandings of humanity to determine gender relationships. Genesis 1 and 2 consistently asserts that all of humanity is made in the image of God. In particular, Genesis 1:27 reveals the importance of both male and female in how humanity reflects the image of God. This passage is written in a tri-colon parallel structure.

So God created man   in his own image,
in the image of God   he created him;
male and female   he created them.

This method of parallelism is a central trait of Hebrew poetry. It repeats the same concept in succeeding lines but with alternative wording. For example, Psalm 148:1 states,

Praise the LORD   from the heavens;
Praise him   in the heights above.

Psalm 148 presents the same concept twice, using parallel phrases: "Praise the LORD"/"Praise him" and "from the heavens"/"in the heights above."

In the Genesis passage, "God created man" is repeated three times using slightly different wording. The second part of the line states that humans were created "in his own image." The specific language of "the image of God" is repeated twice but in the third line is replaced with "male and female." The parallel construction of Genesis 1:27 implies that being created male and female is critical to understanding and appreciating what it means to be made in the image of God.[29] The tri-colon synonymous parallelism of Genesis 1:27 reveals that God's Trinitarian image is reflected in both the male and the female. We can deduce that there is an inherent value and worth to not only the male, but also the female in the capacity to reflect the image of God. Any claim of male spiritual self-sufficiency reflects an arrogant assumption of male adequacy not rooted in the biblical account of creation.

Attempts to diminish or minimize the image of God in women reveal a severe theological dysfunction and sin. Diminishing the image of God in women reflects the sinful tendency to replace God's standards and pronouncements with human standards, which is the basic definition of sin used in this book.

Another example of the misappropriation of Scripture to assert male superiority is found in the interpretation of Genesis 2:18, which states that God made woman to be a "helper" to the man. Often, this passage is used to claim that a woman should be in a subservient role, as a helpful assistant or aide to the man. The Hebrew word for "helper," *ezer*, however, does not mean "helper" in the sense of domestic servitude or a subordinate who helps a superior. Instead *ezer* is "used approximately eighty times in the OT [and] generally indicates military assistance.... This word is generally used to designate divine aid ... The Lord is seen as the helper of the underprivileged: the poor (Ps 72:12) and the fatherless (Ps 10:14; cf. Job 29:12)."[30] In no instance when the word *ezer* is applied to God's relationship to humanity is there any indication that God is subordinate to us. Rather, God helps us because God is greater than us and has a greater capacity to offer help. Therefore, *ezer* claims no sense of inferiority or servitude by the "helper" toward the one who is helped.

The creation account and the doctrine of the image of

God consistently point to the equality of dignity afforded all of humanity. Creation testifies to God's image found in both female and male, and equality that is found not only in what God intended in creation, but also in the equality of human fallenness. A common misinterpretation of the fall places primary blame upon Eve. She is often portrayed as manipulating the situation and luring Adam from afar into the snare of sin. In the actual account, it is explained that Adam was *with* Eve during the interaction with the serpent. Genesis 3:6 states that Eve "also gave some to her husband, *who was with her*, and he ate it" (emphasis added). Both Adam and Eve sinned equally in that moment.

The Genesis account reminds us that all have sinned and continue to fall short of the glory of God. Both male and female and all humanity hold equal responsibility and blame before God. To excuse one group or gender from the full responsibility, or to place greater blame on one group over another, dishonors God's holiness.

Because of our equality in human fallenness, both men and women are redeemed through the same source—Christ. Equality in sin necessitates equality in redemption. Salvation is appropriated equally and in the same manner by both sexes. Ephesians 4:4–6 clearly articulates that "there is one body and one Spirit, just as you were called to one hope when you were called; one Lord, one faith, one baptism; one God and Father of all, who is over all and through all and in all." By elevating the male above the female, we undermine the central tenet of Scripture that we are equal in our dignity in being made in the image of God, equal in our need for redemption because of our human sinfulness, and equal in our salvation that comes from Christ alone. Equality of both male and female before God, therefore, serves as an important theological foundation for understanding biblical anthropology.

While Jesus' work on the cross and his subsequent resurrection confer the dignity of salvation on everyone, his work operates not only in the realm of spiritual redemption but in his human ministry as well. Cultural standards in Jesus' time often demeaned and diminished women, but Jesus, by contrast honored, uplifted, and elevated women above the culture's standards.

In John 4, despite significant cultural restrictions, Jesus engages in a conversation with the Samaritan woman at the well.[31] Jesus affirms the dignity and worth of the individual, even as the culture reduces her to a stereotype and a problem. Jesus sees beyond the cultural and societal definitions and limitations, and engages the full humanity of the Samaritan woman. He affirms her personhood and worth.

Jesus' interaction with the Samaritan woman reveals a consistent ethic. He engages with women and affirms their human dignity and worth, in contrast to the prevailing cultural norms. Jesus befriends Mary and Martha and honors Mary's desire to sit at his feet and learn, a space usually not reserved for women. At the cross, it is women that gather around the suffering servant. And appropriately, women play a central role in discovering the empty tomb. Women play a critical role in the birth, life, ministry, death, and resurrection of Jesus.

The apostle Paul, who is sometimes perceived as a culturally formed individual with misogynistic tendencies, actually demonstrates generosity across the boundaries of gender. His letters to the church often break cultural conventions and expectations as he asserts equality between the genders. Paul emphasizes this sense of equality by stating that in Christ there is neither "male [nor] female, for you are all one in Jesus." (Galatians 3:28). This statement does not imply the absence of differences between the male and female (for example physiological differences), but instead asserts equality deeply rooted in our identity in Christ.

In his letter to the Ephesians, Paul outlines a powerful challenge to the status quo of gender relationships. Ephesians 5:21–33 is part of a genre called "Household Codes," which during the time of Paul often served as a "how-to guide" for families and households. A typical household code of Paul's time would emphasize the role and responsibility of the submissive party within that culture to maintain peace in the household. In other words, the burden of household tranquility rested on the actions of the slave, wife, and child. In contrast, Paul emphasizes the role of the master, husband, and parent in the home. As Craig Keener notes: "Unlike most ancient writers, Paul undermines the basic premise of these codes: the absolute authority of the male head of the house."[32] The dominant group with the power in the culture is challenged toward acts of submission.

This passage in Ephesians reminds us that submission should be mutual rather than one-sided. Ephesians 5:22 is often quoted to emphasize that wives should submit to their husbands. Many wedding sermons have been preached that prioritize the submissive role of the woman based upon this passage. It is often ignored that the verb "to submit" is actually absent in verse 22. Instead, "submit" is implied in verse 22 because it refers back to the verb "submit" used in verse 21.[33] In verse 21, however, submission is not only commanded from the wife toward the husband, but the Scripture requires a mutual submission: "Submit to one another out of reverence for Christ" (5:21).

While the passage continues to discuss other guidelines for households, it opens with the clear necessity of mutual submission. The intention of this interpretation is not to undermine practices that arise from the remaining portion of the text, but to raise the important question of whether the command to mutual submission can be ignored. Is there a willingness to embody the practice of the initial command of mutual submission, which is motivated by our reverence for Christ? Submission, therefore, is a mutual act demanded of all believers and not just specifically for women. Unfortunately, in many evangelical circles, the emphasis is on the submission of the woman to the man while disregarding the call for mutual submission.

As Christians, we have a responsibility to act in accordance with the standards that we find in Scripture. Before calling others to faithful adherence to Scripture, we ourselves should demonstrate that faithful adherence. Before demanding "proper" submissive behavior from others, the Christian should live in accordance to the higher calling outlined in Scripture, even if others do not. Hypocrisy results when we demand from others standards that we ourselves have not lived up to. In gender relationships, greater grace and justice could be embodied if evangelicals would operate under the primary values of Scripture.

Evangelicals are often perceived as hypocrites because of our tendency to tell others what to do while not adhering to our own understanding of the high standards of Scripture. In telling others what to do, we assert our own power and authority, rather than taking the example of Jesus' humility and self-sacrifice. Our priorities reflect the desire to maintain a position of power, rather than seeking full obedience to the text. We replace God's high calling with our own standards.

This brings us to the issue of women speaking in church. One of the coauthors of this book, Soong-Chan, is an ethnic minority male, who has experienced the pain of standing before a Christian gathering and being disempowered by his brothers and sisters because of his race and ethnicity. But even as they dismissed his perspective, they did not challenge his basic right to speak. Though they disagreed with and even demeaned his point of view, very few challenged his right to stand before them as a human being. But a woman's basic right to stand and express her devotion to Christ as one made in the image of God can be undermined by the actions of those who would seek to adhere to the letter of the law and completely vacate the spirit of the law. Turning your back on a woman speaker in church or heckling her is not an act that honors God. Instead, it is a fundamental assault on the humanity of one made in the image of God. Whatever we may believe about the role of women in the church, are we not acting more sinfully in our response than the sin we may believe is being committed?

Our biblical understanding of God's original intention for his created beings challenges the dysfunctional expression of sexism that dishonors the image of God found in all humanity and asserts dominance of one group over another. Furthermore, in contrast to the cultural norms of their time, Jesus' public ministry and Paul's epistles point toward the equal standing of women alongside men before God. Unfortunately, the history of the American church often reveals a demeaning of women, and such dishonoring of God's image results in the church's negative public witness.

The American church often puts forward a public image that contrasts with the biblical model of community and unity. As stated above, Christians often engage in harsh political rhetoric when dealing with this issue. Some in the church may see the expansion of women's roles in society as a problem that must be dealt with by Christians within the church as well as in the public realm. Christians may experience anxiety and discomfort with society's changing gender roles. That anxiety leads to a further entrenchment of the traditional views in response. The theological problem, however, rests not on the freedom of the individual Christian to hold a particular position on gender, but the perspective that seeks to impose that position upon larger society without consideration of other key theological factors. In this schema, the church takes a particular doctrinal position and assumes that it should apply, almost haphazardly, to the whole of secular society.

If the goal is to impose a specific view of gender upon the larger society, the rhetoric often deteriorates into harsh language, which expresses oppression rather than reconciliation. In place of harsh language, Christian political rhetoric should encourage dialogue and conversation. In the zeal to explain certain biblical values (order and authority) in the public realm, we sometimes undermine other important biblical values (grace, peace, community, unity, and unconditional love). To assert male primacy, we undermine the central doctrine of the *imago Dei*.

Christian political rhetoric on the issue of gender tends to favor the strong, rather than the weak. For better or for worse, evangelicals have had a powerful voice in American society, and yet American Christians often see themselves as marginalized from the power structures and systems of our society. Evangelicals often decry that Christian voices are stifled in the public realm even though they have notable power within that system. Evangelicals present a significant voting bloc as well as being a significant economic force. Therefore, harsh rhetoric from evangelicals on the issue of gender does not arise from a marginalized, minority voice, but rather from a position of privilege and power. This power (acknowledged or not) is not being used to advocate for the weak and the oppressed, but rather to retain and perpetuate existing power dynamics and to retain power for the powerful.

In contrast, the message of the gospel and the example of Jesus reveal an all-powerful Messiah who gives up power and assumes a posture of weakness in order to serve the weak. Jesus, who commanded that the little children be allowed to come to him, who sought to affirm the dignity of women, and whose teachings reflected a deep concern and hope for "the very least of these," offers us an example of defending the weak rather than asserting one's own power. But unlike Jesus, the American evangelical church often seeks to extend its own power rather than using its existing power to serve the marginalized. This emphasis on retaining power stands in stark contrast to the example of Scripture.

Signs of Hope and a Prayer of Confession and Lament

John R. Kohlenberger III, a noted biblical scholar, offers a public plea and confession that challenges Christians to reflect on the impact of sexism on the Christian community.

> A product of middle-class suburbia in the '50s and '60s, I was raised in a world well defined by gender based stereotypes. A woman's place was in the home and a real man wouldn't be caught dead doing "women's work," which was less important and less valuable than real work you got paid for. In athletics, I learned not to run or throw like a girl, and when hurt, not to cry like a girl. At home, at school, and at play, I learned boys did things better than girls and men were superior to women.
>
> A product of evangelical education and church affiliation in the '70s and '80s, my secular view of women was not only reinforced, it was sanctified with Scripture. Eve was deceived and corrupted Adam. Sarah lacked Abraham's powerful faith. Jacob's scheming wives were nothing but trouble. Miriam criticized Moses. And don't forget Delilah and Jezebel! It seemed most of the women of the Old Testament were named only to be praised for their physical beauty or vilified for their treacherous dealings with men. From the New Testament, I was taught that women were to be silent and without authority in the church, and were to be absolutely submissive to their husbands in marriage. A standing joke at Bible college and seminary was that women attended only to find a husband, or to learn to teach children.[34]

Kohlenberger confesses, through the very public medium

of a magazine article, his long-term biases and prejudices. He proceeds to offer a biblical reflection that challenges existing sexism in the church. His statement serves as a public confession and a challenge to the church.

Lamentations 1 offers a lament from the perspective of Jerusalem personified as a woman. While speaking as the voice of Daughter Zion, the author describes a kind of suffering that also reflects the very real experiences of women. We offer the lament of Lamentations 1 as a reflection of the voice for women who have suffered because of the sins of the church.

How deserted lies the city,
  once so full of people!
How like a widow is she,
  who once was great among the nations!
She who was queen among the provinces
  has now become a slave.

Bitterly she weeps at night,
  tears are on her cheeks.
Among all her lovers
  there is no one to comfort her.
All her friends have betrayed her;
  they have become her enemies.

After affliction and harsh labor,
  Judah has gone into exile.
She dwells among the nations;
  she finds no resting place.
All who pursue her have overtaken her
  in the midst of her distress.

The roads to Zion mourn,
*   for no one comes to her appointed festivals.*
All her gateways are desolate,
*   her priests groan,*
her young women grieve,
*   and she is in bitter anguish.*

Her foes have become her masters;
*   her enemies are at ease.*
The LORD has brought her grief
*   because of her many sins.*
Her children have gone into exile,
*   captive before the foe.*

All the splendor has departed
*   from Daughter Zion.*
Her princes are like deer
*   that find no pasture;*
in weakness they have fled
*   before the pursuer.*

In the days of her affliction and wandering
*   Jerusalem remembers all the treasures*
*   that were hers in days of old.*
When her people fell into enemy hands,
*   there was no one to help her.*
Her enemies looked at her
*   and laughed at her destruction.*

Jerusalem has sinned greatly
*   and so has become unclean.*
All who honored her despise her,
*   for they have all seen her naked;*
she herself groans
*   and turns away.*

Her filthiness clung to her skirts;
 she did not consider her future.
Her fall was astounding;
 there was none to comfort her.
"Look, LORD, on my affliction,
 for the enemy has triumphed."

The enemy laid hands
 on all her treasures;
she saw pagan nations
 enter her sanctuary —
those you had forbidden
 to enter your assembly.

All her people groan
 as they search for bread;
they barter their treasures for food
 to keep themselves alive.
"Look, LORD, and consider,
 for I am despised."

"Is it nothing to you, all you who pass by?
 Look around and see.
Is any suffering like my suffering
 that was inflicted on me,
that the LORD brought on me
 in the day of his fierce anger?

"From on high he sent fire,
 sent it down into my bones.
He spread a net for my feet
 and turned me back.
He made me desolate,
 faint all the day long.

"My sins have been bound into a yoke;
    by his hands they were woven together.
They have been hung on my neck,
    and the Lord has sapped my strength.
He has given me into the hands
    of those I cannot withstand.

"The Lord has rejected
    all the warriors in my midst;
he has summoned an army against me
    to crush my young men.
In his winepress the Lord has trampled
    Virgin Daughter Judah.

"This is why I weep
    and my eyes overflow with tears.
No one is near to comfort me,
    no one to restore my spirit.
My children are destitute
    because the enemy has prevailed."

Zion stretches out her hands,
    but there is no one to comfort her.
The LORD has decreed for Jacob
    that his neighbors become his foes;
Jerusalem has become
    an unclean thing among them.

"The LORD is righteous,
    yet I rebelled against his command.
Listen, all you peoples;
    look on my suffering.
My young men and young women
    have gone into exile.

"I called to my allies
  but they betrayed me.
My priests and my elders
  perished in the city
while they searched for food
  to keep themselves alive.

"See, LORD, how distressed I am!
  I am in torment within,
and in my heart I am disturbed,
  for I have been most rebellious.
Outside, the sword bereaves;
  inside, there is only death.

"People have heard my groaning,
  but there is no one to comfort me.
All my enemies have heard of my distress;
  they rejoice at what you have done.
May you bring the day you have announced
  so they may become like me.

"Let all their wickedness come before you;
  deal with them
as you have dealt with me
  because of all my sins.
My groans are many
  and my heart is faint."

CHAPTER 5

sins against the LGBTQ community

Historical Reflection

Over the last few decades, the Lesbian, Gay, Bisexual, Transgender, and Queer community (LGBTQ) has been front and center in the so-called culture wars that have marked faith and politics in the United States. One would be hard-pressed to find a group of people that has faced greater consternation and vilification by Christians in the past forty years than gay men and lesbian women. This is partly a result of sweeping social change and a greater acceptance of same-sex attraction in the broader culture. Popular television shows have brought the lives of LGBTQ people into American living rooms. Many Christians now know a friend, neighbor, family member or coworker who has "come out" and let people know that she or he is lesbian or gay. While relationships with people in the LGBTQ community have led many in the church to adopt a more loving approach, others have responded with hate and vitriol.

Meanwhile, politicians and judges have contested the issues in the realm of civil rights: Candidates argue the merits of gay marriage and many states have enacted marriage laws and amendments that restrict marriage to "one man and one woman." The debates and tensions over the definition of marriage and the rights of homosexuals will undoubtedly continue for the foreseeable future. With this backdrop, many journalists and social critics have reason to believe that the most important issue for many Christians and the church in the United States is a concern about homosexuality. Under the banner of protecting marriage, the church has gone on the assault against what is often called the "gay agenda."

Homosexuality is a controversial and at times divisive topic. As we consider the confessions of the church, it is important that we wrestle with some key ways that the church must repent for attitudes and behaviors that have both wounded and demonized the LGBTQ community. After all, at the end of the day, homosexuality is not only or primarily a topic or agenda, but it is about people — millions of people who are precious in God's eyes.

Before the last several decades, while homosexuals rarely revealed their sexual orientation in public and were considered "deviants" by psychologists and religious leaders alike, the relative underground nature of the community meant few Christians explicitly targeted them. Although homosexuals, or "sodomites" (a derogatory term derived from the stories of the destruction of Sodom and Gomorrah in the book of Genesis), were often included in the usual laundry lists of sinners, sexual orientation rarely rose to the level of warranting a sermon theme, let alone a public crusade. The last few decades have more than made up for this, however, as the so-called "gay agenda" has come to define the cultural battle many Christians are waging. Hate-filled rhetoric and attacks on the rights of LGBTQ people have marked this unfortunate period.

The vehement attacks on gays and lesbians have come on the heels of increased willingness of LGBTQ people to "come out" and make their sexual orientation public. Alfred Kinsey's groundbreaking 1948 work, *Sexual Behavior in the Human Male*, argued that many more men are homosexual than previously thought and that there is a continuum between heterosexuality and homosexuality for men. This argument spurred greater concern in the culture and began to bring about greater fear of gays, resulting in more overt prejudice. The Cold War also led to greater attention toward homosexuals, which came to a head in the "Lavender Scare" of the 1950s, when concerns about gays and lesbians were often linked to fears of Communist infiltration. David Johnson asserts that "in 1950, many politicians, journalists, and citizens thought that homosexuals posed more of a threat to national security than Communists." Three of President Harry Truman's advisors suggested as much in a memo to the commander-in-chief that year.[1] The belief that gays and lesbians were "perverted" and "deviant" gave these concerns power in the public imagination. Johnson aptly noted, "Gays, even more than Communists, were phantoms, ciphers upon whom one could project fears about the declining state of America's moral fiber."[2]

In the midst of growing concerns about sexual deviation, LGBTQ identity groups began to emerge, including the Mattachine Society. These groups fostered conversations about how to become a more accepted part of American society.

One event above all others catapulted many in the LGBTQ community into the public arena in an effort to pursue civil rights and protections: Stonewall. During the summer of 1969, an early morning raid of the Stonewall Inn, a gay bar located in Greenwich Village in New York City, sparked two days of unrest, protests, and violence between police and gay men over their ill-treatment during the raid.

The greater focus on legal rights and protections began to draw the attention of some in the Christian community. Organized protests by gay rights groups coupled with new findings in the field of psychology led the board of trustees of the American Psychiatric Association to no longer classify homosexuality as a mental disorder in their industry standard *Diagnostic and Statistical Manual of Mental Disorders*.

In response, many Christians prepared for battle, and one of the first skirmishes took place in the Miami metro area.[3] In the mid-1970s, communities around the country were debating the issue of civil rights for homosexuals. After the county commissioners in Dade County, Florida, passed a gay-rights bill in 1977, a new organization called Save Our Children formed. The new group, founded by former Miss America runner-up Anita Bryant, included many conservative Christians. At the new organization's founding press conference, local Miami clergy supported Bryant, who claimed that homosexuals were actively "trying to recruit our children to homosexuality." Save Our Children, which claimed gays and lesbians were a direct threat to children, successfully overturned the county commissioner's gay-rights bill in a landslide vote.[4]

Bryant, in her 1977 book, *The Anita Bryant Story*, leveled the charge that homosexuals seeking civil rights were leading America toward a corporate disease: "There are homosexual adults who are living irresponsibly, who in the name of 'human rights' seek social rights that in reality only give them license for perversion and the flaunting of their deviant ways. To allow this to continue is only an indication that rather than being a great society, we are a sick society."[5] Bryant later added, "A society that condones homosexual behavior is a society that is uncaring, for it is allowing an individual to fall prey to sexual self-destruction."[6]

Following the victory, Bryant set her sights on overturning gay-rights bills across the nation. She found quick support from the new vanguard of the burgeoning religious right, including Jerry Falwell, Jim and Tammy Bakker, and Pat Robertson.[7] Together, the Moral Majority and its heir, the Christian Coalition, elected to adopt Bryant's battle as one of the epic struggles of what they believed was a culture war between good and evil, Christian and pagan.

The name of Bryant's nascent organization, Save Our Children, spoke to a common attitude of the culture warriors: The American family, they felt, was under attack, and the most vulnerable were most at risk. Bryant made the latent threat that she believed gays posed to children very explicit: "Homosexuals cannot reproduce—so they must recruit. And to freshen their ranks, they must recruit the youth of America."[8] Bryant expressed specific concerns about the possibility of having gay teachers in the public schools: "Known homosexual schoolteachers and their possible role-model impact tore at my heart in a way I could not ignore. Two things in particular troubled me. First, public approval of admitted homosexual teachers could encourage more homosexuality by inducing pupils into looking upon it as an acceptable lifestyle. And second, a particularly deviant-minded teacher could sexually molest children."[9] For Bryant and many of her colleagues, homosexuals were recast as pariahs directly threatening good Christian children.

This mistaken inference that homosexuals tend to be child molesters has become all-too-common when Christians have talked about sexual orientation over the past several decades. In fact, one of the most common charges leveled by Christians against homosexuals has been they prey on children. Oregon Citizens Alliance president Lon Mabon, as he worked to cultivate an effort to deny civil rights protections for homosexuals in his state in the early 1990s, argued that the acceptance of homosexuality would inevitably lead to an acceptance of pedophilia by the end of the twentieth century.[10]

This trend did not end as we entered the new millennium. In response to the recent scandal involving Penn State assistant football coach Jerry Sandusky, Dr. James Dobson included a recognition of over one hundred thirty Southern Baptist clergy who have been accused of sexually abusing children, and also referenced the Catholic sex-abuse scandals of recent years. He sums up the paragraph by asserting, "Most of those heinous acts were performed by homosexual pedophiles."[11] The truth is that heterosexuals also sexually abuse children and that the overwhelming majority of LGBTQ people are horrified and saddened by pedophilia. Such "Save Our Children" rhetoric is both unfair and untrue.

In the early 1980s, word spread of a new disease that primarily affected and killed homosexuals. Some labeled the growing epidemic the Gay Plague, or the Gay Immune Deficiency Syndrome. It was common for Christians to suggest that the disease, which would come to be called AIDS (Auto-Immune Deficiency Syndrome), represented God's judgment on LGBTQ people. Christians failed miserably to respond with love and grace when the HIV/AIDS epidemic first hit. Rev. Jerry Falwell, who established the Moral Majority in the late 1970s, was not alone among evangelical Christians when he claimed, "AIDS is not just God's punishment for homosexuals. It is God's punishment for the society that tolerates homosexuals."[12] At a time of great suffering and fear in the LGBTQ community, Christians had an opportunity to demonstrate the love and compassion demonstrated in Jesus' parable of the Good Samaritan. Instead, many not only passed by on the other side of the road but rhetorically spat upon the suffering AIDS victim lying on the side of the Jericho Road.

Occasionally, blinded by fear and hate, Christians lose sight of their Lord's core commandment: Love your neighbor. In April 1989, over thirty Florida Baptist ministers presented an award of merit to Judge Susan Skinner who had earned their praise for forcing a person with AIDS to leave her courtroom a few months earlier. Instead of condemning this type of bigotry and hate, the clergy celebrated the renegade magistrate. Reverend Richard Riley of Emmanuel Baptist Church in Ft. Myers went so far as to say of Judge Skinner's actions: "We thought that was admirable."[13] While this type of insensitivity was never the norm for Christians, these types of episodes are common enough that many in the gay community saw conservative Christians as the enemy.

Over the past decade, the fear and hatred of people with HIV/AIDS has dropped substantially in the church as congregations have focused on the devastating effects of the disease in Africa and other parts of the world. The concern for women and orphans whose lives have been devastated by HIV in poorer nations is laudable. Still, the church has by and large failed to ever apologize for its insensitivity and vilification of AIDS victims and for using this horrific disease as an opportunity to bash LGBTQ people.

In the 1990s, as the focus on AIDS being a God-ordained judgment on homosexuals began to wane, attention again turned to local struggles over gay-rights initiatives and battles over civil unions and gay marriage for homosexuals. In the mid-1990s, a Republican-controlled Congress partnered with Democratic President Bill Clinton to pass the Defense of Marriage Act, which defined marriage as a commitment between "one man and one woman." This did not prevent state supreme courts from weighing in on the subject, and highly contentious state-wide marriage amendments showed up across the country. While these legal and legislative skirmishes continue, an unfortunate constant has been rhetoric that demonizes gays. A Florida preacher, quoted in a 1993 *Orlando Sentinel* article, had this over-the-top response to the perceived danger posed by LGBTQ people: "They are like rats, skulking in their closets, circulating in mad frenzies, unable to control their sexual appetites, sniffing around the doors of school classrooms for fresh prey. Young prey. They are perverts and hedonists and spread disease like rats once spread the Black Plague. They will make fine kindling in Hell. But before then, before God gives them what they really deserve, they must be stopped here on earth."[14] This type of rhetoric is not common, but it points to the dehumanizing impulses that some in the Christian community have allowed to enter their consciousness. Such rhetoric violates the central teachings of Scripture that all people are created in God's image and are precious in God's eyes.

Not even two years into the twenty-first century, the horrific events of 9/11 changed the trajectory of the nation and the world. Unfortunately, it took only two days for Jerry Falwell and Pat Robertson to lay at least part of the blame for the tragedy on the LGBTQ people and those who tolerate them. On Robertson's television program, *The 700 Club*, Falwell said, "I really believe that the pagans, and the abortionists, and the feminists, and the gays and lesbians who are actively trying to make that an alternative lifestyle, the ACLU, People for the American Way—all of them who have tried to secularize America—I point the finger in their face and say, 'You helped make this happen.'" Robertson admitted that he agreed with the sentiment.[15]

This knee-jerk attempt to blame those who are perceived as unrighteous, and the LGBTQ community in particular, for natural disasters and acts of terror speaks to the overall dehumanization of gays and lesbians that has been going on for decades. The all-too-common Christian rhetoric has been that gays are threatening our children, our families, our culture, and even our nature. They are deviants and therefore dangerous, and consequently blamed and even dehumanized in the process. This regrettable history of hate demands confession and repentance.

Theological Reflections

Romans 3:23 serves as a critical verse for American Christian doctrine. Explanations of the gospel message often begin by citing this verse, which reminds us that *all* have sinned and fall short of the glory of God. Paul asserts the universality of human sinfulness in the first phrase (*all* have sinned) and amplifies this assertion by using the present tense for the verb *fall*.

John Stott argues that the phrase "for all have sinned" asserts "everybody's cumulative past [is] being summed up by an aorist tense" and that the phrase "fall short" reflects "a continuing present."[16] In other words, there is also a unity of sinfulness that comes from the entirety of our sinful history. There is a unity of sinfulness in the continuous falling short of God's glory. The common state of sinfulness of all humanity is a central doctrine of evangelical faith. The gift and blessing of being created in the image of God is balanced with the reality of our fallen sinful nature. The doctrine of original sin reminds us that no one stands innocent before God.

Romans 3 reminds us that the common reality of human sinfulness is measured against the glory of God. Our ongoing and continuous falling short of God's glory derives from the immutability of God's holiness and righteousness. God's righteousness remains constant and our falling short reflects the truth of God's constant holiness. Despite our best human attempts, the holiness of an immutable and unchanging God can never be attained.

A sinful tendency in the American church is the imposition of a human scale for sin over and against God's ordering of sin. Many Christians identify homosexuality as a sin. Others question that identification, but this chapter won't engage that debate. Instead, it will focus on how we as Christians have operated within that identification. As stated, the LGBTQ community is "a group that has faced the most vilification" from the evangelical community. Evangelicals have moved far beyond simply identifying homosexuality as a violation of Scriptures' tenets into extreme vilification. Recent evangelical responses to the LGBTQ community reveal the human propensity toward ongoing sinfulness and how much we continue to fall short of the glory of God. In our ongoing act of demonizing the LGBTQ community, human sinfulness is repeatedly enacted.

The human attempt to impose gradations of sin based on human standards reflects an act of sin itself. Human standards usurp God's standards. As stated in chapter 3, a theological definition of sin is the attempt to place human beings as the standard for righteousness and holiness. This attempt usurps God's rightful place in creation.

Evangelical theology operates from certain key intellectual assumptions. Historian George Marsden points out that "Scottish Common Sense" philosophy plays a prominent role in the formation of evangelical theology. That philosophy operates under certain assumptions. As Marsden summarizes, "According to Common Sense philosophy, one can intuitively know the first principles of morality as certainly as one can apprehend other essential aspects of reality."[17] In other words, a theology founded upon Common Sense philosophy is simply biased toward one's own point of view. If evangelicals assume that a divinely sanctioned Common Sense shapes one's point of view, then there is an underlying assumption that one's point of view is intuitively and correctly derived. Therefore, the perspective arising out of the rational mindset stands as the most accurate one.

To challenge Common Sense philosophy is not to assert that truth cannot be understood. Rather, the biblical challenge is to not assume that our Common Sense assumptions are absolutely correct. The danger of Common Sense philosophy is to attribute non-negotiable status to our enlightenment assumptions. If Common Sense becomes the measure of our biblical faith, then our rational assumptions can take the place of God's ordering of creation.

This enlightenment approach to sin usually favors the dominant culture's narrative within the evangelical church and does not allow for a nuanced interpretation of sin. In other words, the dominant culture within evangelicalism has the authority to gauge and determine sin through the lens of personal assumptions rather than Scripture.

The individual that follows the line of reasoning offered by evangelical doctrine could get the wrong impression that their perspective (presumably obtained using reason and logic) produces the definitive position for the entire community that perfectly mirrors the biblical perspective. Since the individual gained this understanding through reason and logic, all other options can be eliminated. If the evangelical understanding of a specific sin is derived from following a line of reasoning, then that particular sin would hold a greater primacy. There is minimal consideration for the possibility of an intrinsic bias because of our assumption that our reasoning trumps our bias.

This approach leads to a disproportionate emphasis on specific sins. Robert Putnam notes that American Christianity tends to emphasize sexual sins above other expressions of sin.[18] Evangelicals often ignore social sins such as economic injustice and corporate acts of violence, which are sin in the eyes of God every bit as much as acts of sexual immorality. Our ordering of sin often reveals the priorities of the culture more than the actual priorities of Scripture. For example, why do evangelicals usually not put as much energy into challenging our idolatry of American capitalism as they do toward demonizing the LGBTQ community?

While most evangelicals ably identify blatant sins, they have difficulty recognizing more hidden, diabolical sins. Such sins usually operate from a motivation of pride. Sin can emerge from even a well-intentioned move toward holiness, if that attempt is infused with arrogance. C. S. Lewis identifies that the source of this pride is not godly. Lewis asserts, "Whenever we find that our religious life is making us feel that we are good—above all, that we are better than someone else—I think we may be sure that we are being acted on, not by God, but by the devil."[19]

Diabolical sin assumes the superiority of one's own perspective over another's. It accommodates the power to uphold one's own position and standing as definitive over and above other positions. It affirms the arrogance of evangelical assumptions about the nature, intensity, and gradation of sin. Arrogance leads to the assumption that we have figured out which sins are more important than others. This perspective challenges Jesus' words that "he who is without sin [should] cast the first stone."

Diabolical sin allows evangelical Christianity to stand in an elevated position and cast aspersions on those it deems less worthy. The pride that underlies diabolical sin also leads to the assumption that others are worthy of judgment, but not us. During the 2008 presidential campaign, Focus on the Family offered extreme and dire predictions if Barack Obama were to be elected. Most of those doom-and-gloom scenarios failed to materialize, but after the reelection of Barack Obama in

2012, many Christians were still hammering away at that doom-and-gloom scenario.

Some evangelicals are particularly concerned that God's judgment will fall upon the United States for tolerating homosexuality. What is seldom taken into consideration is the reality of widespread heterosexual sin — in all probability at a much higher rate. Homosexual sin committed on a smaller scale is deemed worthy of God's wrath, but other sins, even other sexual sins, do not receive as much attention.

Even as evangelicals engage in categorizing sin, there is also a level of selectivity in how we use political influence. An additional important theological consideration in our corporate confession of how we have treated the LGBTQ community is how we view the role of the church in the context of a secular state; specifically, is it the role of the church to legislate morality in a secular democracy like ours?

For most of the twentieth century, American evangelicals disengaged from the larger culture. Secular culture was seen as a wrecked vessel that should be abandoned to the judgment of God. In the process of disengagement, the church remained silent on a number of issues, including the Civil Rights movement and concern for the poor and the disenfranchised of our society. Evangelicals chose a level of separation from what was perceived to be the most evil aspects of society.

In the last quarter of the twentieth century, evangelicals reengaged society on particular political issues such as opposition to abortion, US support for Israel, and opposition to same-sex marriage. While a healthy desire not to abandon the culture should be acknowledged, the question needs to be raised whether this type of evangelical social and political engagement was an appropriate response. Evangelicals ended up seeking to establish laws that only furthered the comfort level of the privileged. Evangelical political power attempted to apply evangelical norms of morality and the proper ordering of society to everyone. How did evangelicals end up wanting only to protect our own position of privilege and power rather than seeking to protect the innocent, the marginalized, and disenfranchised?

To what extent should evangelicals favor specific moral concerns over their responsibility to "the very least of these?" Of course evangelicals should have the freedom to determine jurisdiction over our own policy, and the healthy separation of church and state allows for this. But should there be limits to how they apply the morality they direct toward their own believing community as opposed to how they apply that morality over the entire secular state? Imposing standards of individual morality on the secular society results in a picking and choosing of certain pet issues, issues which may not be applicable to the larger community.

The evangelical community's venom and vitriol directed against the LGBTQ community is in violation of God's commands to love your neighbor as yourself. By substituting human gradations of sin over God's standards, evangelicals reveal an animosity toward homosexuals that is not appropriate for the Christian community. Our sins of excessive vilification, grading sin, and absence of concern for others for the sake of our own comfort reminds us that we have all sinned and continue to fall short of the glory of God.

Signs of Hope and a Prayer of Confession and Lament

Pastor Jer Swigart leads the Open Door Community, a progressive young church, in Walnut Creek, California, only twenty-five miles away from San Francisco. The church community is defined by what it means to live like Jesus by sharing his love with the world. For years they have been globally connected. One of their mission partners focuses on responding to the needs of men, women, and children suffering from HIV/AIDS in Uganda. However, as the church has developed relationships and sought to respond to the needs they were seeing, they also began to ask the question, "How much of a right do we have to care about global AIDS when we are not showing up to respond to the needs of people affected by AIDS locally?"

As a result, Swigart decided to learn more about the effects of AIDS in the San Francisco area. On December 1, 2008, accompanied by his one-year-old daughter, he attended the National AIDS Memorial Grove gathering to commemorate the lives of those affected by the disease. There he encountered a stark reality. AIDS in San Francisco did not look like the widows and the orphans he had met in Uganda. Rather, AIDS in the Bay Area looked like "you and me"; young Americans from different cultures and backgrounds deeply affected by AIDS. During this encounter, Swigart realized that two things were clearly missing from this AIDS commemoration gathering: first, hope, and second, the Christian community. Convicted and compelled, he returned to his church community and began to gather a small group of people to join the AIDS Memorial Grove community once a month at their community work days to do landscaping and other projects in the community. He says, "We just started to show up—over and over—intentionally developing relationships."

The following year, the AIDS Memorial Grove community was having a fundraising event called "Light in the Grove." As they planned for the event, they realized the only way they would be able to pull it off and still be able to raise some money was if they could get a substantial group of volunteers to support the event. Who did they call? Their friends at the Open Door Community. Swigart and Open Door embraced the opportunity to serve and prayed that they would fully take on "every role of the servant." Now, almost four years later, the relationships between Open Door and the AIDS Memorial Grove community are significant. In 2012, during an anniversary to host their covenant partners, the National AIDS Memorial Grove identified three communities that have come alongside of them in support and solidarity: Wells Fargo Bank, a local high school which has been participating in their workdays for decades, and the Open Door community.

When Swigart was asked what he had learned from this partnership, he said that Open Door had learned firsthand how HIV/AIDS had "ravaged the gay community in San Francisco." They learned what it means to live out God's love by offering a "radical embrace" to a community that has been often marginalized and stigmatized by the Christian church. Swigart describes his church as an evangelical Christian community that seeks to honor Jesus by doing the "subversive work of developing friendships." The goal is not for Christians to enter into relationships in order to "fix" people, but rather to reshape the paradigm of missions and point others to Jesus and his salvation through a posture of holistic engagement and authentic relationship. For Swigart and the Open Door community, these relationships are what it means to "embrace the reality of Jesus."[20]

A prayer of confession and lament

Lord Jesus, forgive us for our attitude toward sexuality,
when we have not honored you as our divine Creator.
Forgive us for the ways we have undermined sexuality
by treating it as sin ... Forgive us for the ways we have
elevated male over female or over those with differing
gender identification ... Forgive us for the way we have

related to lesbian, gay, bisexual, transgender, and queer people as subhuman. We beg your forgiveness for how we have hurt people who suffer from gender confusion. We beg your forgiveness for the ways we, as Christians, often treat people who are practicing gays. We have sinned against you by demonizing and being overtly hateful to the LGBTQ community.
Forgive us.[21]

CHAPTER 6

sins against immigrants

Historical Overview

One of the enduring symbols of American identity is the Statue of Liberty. Located near Ellis Island, the gateway for countless European immigrants to the United States, "Lady Liberty" is inscribed with a poem by Emma Lazarus titled "The New Colossus." Written as a tribute to the statue and the nation, the poem famously concludes:

> Give me your tired, your poor,
> Your huddled masses yearning to breathe free,
> The wretched refuse of your teeming shore.
> Send these, the homeless, tempest-tost to me,
> I lift my lamp beside the golden door![1]

The story that Americans tell ourselves is that we are a

nation of immigrants. Many of us embrace the metaphor of a melting pot to capture the nation's ability to receive and assimilate those who were born elsewhere. For those Americans who can chart their family trees back to Ellis Island, or, better yet, to the Puritans of New England or the first settlers of Virginia, an immigrant heritage is a badge of honor.

Most Americans, however, do not share this old immigration legacy, and even those who do have forgotten the real challenges faced by their ancestors when they first graced the shores of New York, New England, or Virginia. This narrative erases the Native American population that the newcomers pushed aside in waves, and it glosses over the forced immigration of millions of African Americans as slaves. In addition, this story fails to acknowledge the recurring pattern of US citizens vilifying those newly arrived from Ireland, Germany, Southern and Eastern Europe, Africa, Asia, and Latin America. In many instances, Christians not only failed to welcome immigrants; at times some in the Protestant church even led the effort to attack and demonize immigrants.

Throughout US history there have been seasons of anti-immigrant fervor, beginning with the presidency of John Adams, when Congress passed the highly controversial Alien and Sedition Acts of 1798. The legislation targeted French immigrants as being suspect and dangerous to the security of the young republic. Although these measures were harshly criticized in the years following, a general suspicion of "aliens" and immigrants has reemerged in the US time and again.

One part of the anti-French feeling in the late eighteenth century was the general suspicion of Catholics. The largely Protestant colonists, and particularly the Puritans, still retained much of their British anti-Catholic bias, tendencies that came to fruition from the 1830s through the 1850s, during the Second Great Awakening and while portions of the church were deeply involved in the abolitionist movement.[2] Ironically, many of those who advocated an end to slavery were also the most biased against Catholic immigrants from Ireland and Germany. The American Bible Society, an organization founded to distribute Bibles and fight slavery, was just one of many tract societies of the day that forged part of its identity and mission from an opposition to Catholicism.[3]

The one book most associated with the abolitionist cause is, of course, Harriett Beecher Stowe's *Uncle Tom's Cabin*, a novel that sought to expose the horrors of slavery. Stowe did some of her research while living in Cincinnati, Ohio. She had moved there in the 1830s with her father, the renowned minister Lyman Beecher, who had elected to leave his prestigious church in Boston to become president of Lane Theological Seminary. Beecher, perhaps the most popular preacher in the United States at the time, became convinced that the battle for the soul of America would be won or lost in the West. While his daughter worked for the abolitionist cause, he was focused on the perceived threat of Catholicism. Concerned that Catholic immigrants had a head start on the frontier, the elder Beecher elected to go West himself to do all he could for the Protestant cause. His characterization of many immigrants as "infidels" in his essay "A Plea for the West" tapped into America's anti-immigrant impulses. Beecher's hope was that through Lane Seminary, Protestant orthodoxy would battle and ultimately triumph over the decaying influence of the immigrant population, including their heretical Catholicism.[4]

Beecher regularly raised money for the seminary by stressing the urgency of the hour. In August 1834, during a time of extreme anxiety over alleged corruption within Catholic monasteries and convents, Beecher delivered extremely harsh anti-Catholic sermons in three different Boston churches in one evening. The very next night a group of ruffians took it upon themselves to burn down the Ursuline Convent in nearby Charleston, the most prominent convent in the region. The arsonists cheered as the building went up flames, amid shouts of "No popery" and "Down with the cross."[5] The anti-immigrant violence did not end there. The next day, the rumor spread that groups of Irish Catholics were preparing to descend upon Boston to seek their revenge. In what they justified as a pre-emptive strike, a group of Protestants attacked a shanty that housed nearly forty Irish laborers, burning it to the ground.[6] Although on the following Sunday Beecher condemned these acts of arson as atrocities, his vitriolic rhetoric had already done its damage.[7]

Like Beecher, the popular preacher Horace Bushnell also raised grave concerns about the threat of immigrants to the American way of life. In 1837 Bushnell offered these remarks: "The constant importation, as now, to this country, of the lowest orders of people from abroad, to dilute the quality of our natural manhood, is a sad and beggarly prostitution of the noblest gift ever conferred on a people. Who shall respect a people, who shall not respect their own blood?"[8] Bushnell dismissed immigrants from Germany and Ireland as a threat to the purity of the American race. This type of bigoted and anti-immigrant rhetoric, laced with racist undertones, mirrors the type of ugly language that often flowed from the lips of Christians throughout this nation's history.

The anti-Catholicism of the 1830s gave way to full-fledged attacks on immigrants, particularly those from Ireland and Germany, in the 1840s. Increasingly, Protestants began to stereotype immigrants as poverty stricken, relying disproportionately on public assistance, and exhibiting gross immorality, violent crime, and drunkenness.[9] Following the economic panic of 1837, jobs became scarce, which led many to accuse immigrants of taking jobs from American citizens.[10]

The fear and growing hatred of immigrants sometimes manifested itself in unusual public battles. In Philadelphia in 1844, for instance, a group of over ninety clergy responded to a demand by Catholic Bishop Francis Patrick Kenrick that Catholic school children not be required to read the King James Version of the Bible in school. The Protestant pastors issued a public statement, denouncing the threat posed to the nation "from the assaults of Romanism." Shortly thereafter, anti-immigrant and anti-Catholic riots occurred, leading to the torching of several homes as well as two Catholic churches, and to the deaths of several Irish immigrants.[11]

Christian opposition to immigrants soon found institutional expression. In June 1848 the American Protestant Society entered an agreement with the Christian Alliance to work to convert American Catholics. The following year, the Christian Union, the Foreign Evangelical Society, and the American Protestant Society merged to form the American and Foreign Christian Union to further a Protestant agenda in the United States and around the world.[12] Attempts to evangelize and proselytize are paramount for people of many faiths, including Protestants and Catholics. This alone is not necessarily cause for alarm. But all too often during this era, such a Protestant agenda meant an anti-immigrant agenda.

In the 1850s, after years of increased immigration from Ireland and Germany, religious newspapers joined a growing chorus of voices taking aim at new arrivals. Nearly every day, these papers cited a litany of statistics and stories illustrating the elevated rates of poverty and crime in municipalities throughout the nation and placed the blame squarely on immigrants.[13] Christian institutions, schools, and media formed a coordinated effort to stem the immigrant Catholic tide.

The anti-immigrant fervor culminated in the ascendency of the Know Nothing Party of the mid 1850s, so named because the members, when asked about their party affiliation, would claim that they knew nothing. For a few years, sandwiched between the downfall of the Whig Party and the emergence of the Republican Party, the Know Nothing Party rode anti-immigrant rhetoric to a modicum of political power.[14]

In the 1850s, some even suspected that Abraham Lincoln was sympathetic toward the Know Nothing Party, though Lincoln's response was firm: "How could I be? How can anyone who abhors the oppression of negroes be in favor of degrading classes of white people?" Imagining a future in which anti-immigrant forces might take power, the future president believed the slogan that "all men are created equal" would become "all men are created equal, except negroes, and foreigners and Catholics."[15] Lincoln recognized the underlying tone of white Protestant supremacy that informed the anti-immigrant movement, and in private correspondence he distanced himself from any affiliation with such sentiments. After a brief rise to prominence, the Know Nothing Party, with its anti-immigrant emphasis, would take a backseat to Abraham Lincoln, abolition, slavery, and the Civil War.

By about 1870, however, some people were again paying attention to the issue of immigration. In that year, Senator Charles Sumner proposed an amendment to the Constitution that would eliminate the word "white" from all acts of Congress dealing with immigration, naturalization, or citizenship, effectively asserting the equality of all nations and races. In response, a senator from Oregon wanted assurances that such an amendment would still prohibit the Chinese immigrants from becoming citizens. Another senator, half-jokingly, suggested that the amendment be passed "provided that the provisions of this act shall not apply to persons born in Asia, Africa, or any of the islands of the Pacific, nor to any Indians born in the wilderness."[16] In the years just before the completion of the

Statue of Liberty, which sought to convey a message of welcome to European immigrants, those from other parts of the world were increasingly discouraged from coming to America.

While the nation grew slowly more comfortable with Irish and German immigrants, they adamantly refused to accept Chinese immigrants. They conveniently ignored the fact that Western expansion depended in part on the Chinese immigrants who helped build thousands of miles of railroad tracks. When railway jobs dried up and the economy experienced a downturn, these Chinese immigrants became convenient scapegoats, and lawmakers proposed and often passed harsh anti-Chinese legislation in the 1880s, including the Chinese Exclusion Act and the Alien Contract Labor Laws.[17] Congress would later approve legislation outlawing Asians, including a restriction on Japanese immigration, in 1907 and 1908.[18]

During this same period, others were concerned about the large numbers of Southern and Eastern Europeans entering the nation through New York City. Even church leaders and clergy affiliated with the progressive Social Gospel movement had reservations about this vast influx of immigrants. Josiah Strong was one of the leading voices of the Social Gospel Movement, which emphasized the need for social transformation and progress in addition to individual salvation. In 1885, Strong wrote the popular *Our Country: Its Possible Future and Its Present Crisis*. A pastor who called for greater missionary zeal and more ardent responses to social problems, Strong also accepted white superiority and echoed attacks on non-Anglo immigrants.[19] He saw a coming class conflict between rich and poor and believed that this threat was exacerbated by increased immigration.[20] Strong, who served as secretary of the Evangelical Society of the United States, also argued that Catholic immigrants were a threat to American citizens.[21]

In his book, Strong argues that "there can be no reasonable

doubt that North America is to be the great home of the Anglo-Saxon, the principal seat of his power, the center of his life and influence." Strong's words regarding immigrants were even more vitriolic: "The typical immigrant is a European peasant, whose horizon has been narrow, whose moral and religious training has been meager or false, and whose ideas of life are low. Not a few belong to the pauper and criminal classes." He further argued that immigrants were "transplanted from a forest to an open prairie, where before he is rooted, he is smitten with blasts of temptation," later adding, "Our population of foreign extraction is sadly conspicuous in our criminal records."[22]

Jacob Riis, another advocate of the Social Gospel, argued in his book *How the Other Half Lives* that only a stringent commitment to Christian justice could limit the increasing gulf between rich and poor spurred on by the greed of the wealthiest. As he explored the conditions facing the poor, Riis painted a picture of the horrific conditions often found in tenements populated by immigrants. His thick descriptions of squalor in tenement houses, while written out of compassion, reinforced stereotypes and furthered an anti-immigrant spirit.[23] Another member of the Protestant clergy, Reverend Justin D. Fuller of Boston, penned several alarmist books chronicling the supposed danger of Catholic immigrants. His works, which included *Rome in America* (1887), warned of the growth of Catholic organizations and institutions in the United States.[24]

Even Social Gospel leader Walter Rauschenbusch, who lobbied in favor of German immigration, occasionally derided the quality of immigrants coming from other parts of the world. During a 1905 fund-raising appeal for Rochester University's German department, Rauschenbusch asked, "Are the whites of this continent so sure of their possession against the blacks of the South and the seething yellow flocks beyond the Pacific that they need no reinforcement of men of their own blood while yet it is time?" A few years earlier, Rauschenbusch called for Anglo-Saxons to guard and protect democracy from "alien strains" who were immigrating to the nation from around the world.[25]

These progressive clergy were joined by many stalwarts within the Women's Christian Temperance Union (WCTU) in challenging the vast numbers of new immigrants, particularly from Eastern and Southern Europe. In their efforts to outlaw alcohol, they portrayed the saloon industry as an alien and foreign enterprise. They even claimed that a full 87 percent of saloon owners were "foreigners." The WCTU played upon fears of immigrants in order to advance their agenda against alcohol.[26]

More conservative Protestants also joined the anti-immigrant parade. Revivalist Billy Sunday, perhaps the most popular evangelist of his era, attributed many of the problems facing the country in the 1920s and 1930s to immigrants and "aliens." Acknowledging that the nation was often considered the world's "melting pot," Sunday said it was "time to skim off the scum." Although Sunday claimed he had no problem with immigrants who were ready and willing to assimilate quickly, he also proclaimed, "If they don't like the way we run our own country, then I say let them take their damnable carcasses and get back to where they came from."[27]

Many working Americans began to parrot the rhetoric of pastors and organizations like the WCTU. Beginning in 1915, the Ku Klux Klan reemerged with a strong anti-immigrant agenda. To belong to the Klan during its rebirth in the early twentieth century, one had to be white, Gentile, born in the United States, not a Catholic, and ready to defend Protestant Christianity.[28] Hiram Wesley Evans, who became the Imperial Wizard of the Klan, embraced the motto: "Native, White, Protestant Supremacy!" A study of the reach of the Klan in

Youngstown, Ohio, revealed that around a third of the region's Methodists and one fourth of the area's Presbyterians were active in the Klan. Similar alarming statistics were recorded in Pennsylvania and Indiana.[29]

This cacophony of anti-immigrant voices responded to very real demographic changes within the United States. Between 1840 and 1910, the number of Catholics in the nation grew exponentially. In 1840, there were roughly 650,000 Catholics in the country. Seventy years later, that number had mushroomed to around 12 million. In less than a century, the Catholic population had grown nearly twenty-fold.[30]

Many white Protestants responded with fear and resorted to charged rhetoric that eventually led to new anti-immigrant legislation. These new laws, which began to significantly regulate the numbers of immigrants to the United States for the first time, were based on prescribed quotas that favored Western European immigrants while suppressing or eliminating entry from other parts of the world.

In 1914 Reverend Sidney L. Gulick, in his book *The American Japanese Problem*, proposed what he deemed a "nondiscriminatory" quota system that would allow future immigrants based on an agreed upon percentage of those already in the United States from that particular nation. Even though Gulick was a former missionary to Japan who longed for better relationships between the Eastern and Western worlds, he still believed that "the proved capacity for genuine Americanization on the part of those already here from any land should be the measure for the future immigration of that people."[31] His proposals and others like them helped shape a framework for immigration restrictions that emerged in the 1920s. Obviously, these restrictions granted privilege to those seeking to immigrate from Northern and Western Europe.

In 1921, President Warren Harding signed legislation

limiting new immigrants to the United States based on their nationality by only allowing three percent of the number of foreign born from that country who were in the United States in 1910 to enter. So if there were 100,000 people in the US Census of 1910 who were born in Spain, then only 3,000 from Spain could enter the US in any year.[32] A few years later, in 1924, President Calvin Coolidge signed the Johnson-Reed Act. This law further limited the number of immigrants from Southern and Eastern Europe while effectively eliminating most Asians. The Johnson-Reed Act set quotas based on percentages from a particular ethnicity rather than those born in other countries, and set the baseline numbers on the 1890 Census, until the year 1927. This time, 2 percent would be allowed in, so if there were 2,000,000 of Irish descent in the nation in 1890, 40,000 would be allowed to come into the US each year. From 1927 and thereafter, the total number of immigrants would be set at 150,000 per year, with percentages determined by ethnic origins as calculated in the 1920 Census. This act not only limited immigration from Eastern and Southern Europe but also prohibited all Asian immigration except for a small number from the Philippines.[33]

Following the passage of the Johnson-Reed act, concerns about Mexican immigrants emerged in a significant way for the first time. Since the Johnson-Reed Act did not restrict immigration within the Western Hemisphere, Mexicans and others from Central America could continue to immigrate without significant restrictions. Still, to enter the United States legally, they had to pass through checkpoints, pay fees, and endure health inspections. Many chose to avoid the barriers, which one observer at the time referred to as "locked doors surrounded by open space."[34] Often poorer Mexicans desiring to enter the country had to endure showers from high-pressure hoses, delousing, and were forced to be naked during inspections.[35]

These dehumanizing and humiliating conditions led many Mexicans entering the US for seasonal work to go around the checkpoints.

What followed was a new designation in American parlance: the undocumented or "illegal" immigrant. Concerned about Asians entering the country through Mexico or the funneling of alcohol and other narcotics into the nation during Prohibition, government authorities began to periodically send out teams to find and deport undocumented immigrants. These new laws of the 1920s meant that for the first time in the history of the United States, borders and national sovereignty became the dominant issue in immigration law, instead of the demand for labor, the need for assimilation, freedom from tyranny or oppression abroad, or family unity.[36]

Another growing feature of anti-immigrant sentiment in the twentieth century was anti-Semitism. On June 8, 1939, the New York State Chamber of Commerce published a racist and anti-immigrant report by Harry Laughlin called *Conquest by Immigration*. Laughlin was a leading proponent of sterilization for less desirable people in order to improve the "stock" of Americans, and his ideas were part of the inspiration for the large sterilization program in Nazi Germany. The report argued that because Jews were included among the Poles and Germans, the United States had already allowed more than the allotted share of Jews into the country. The report, however, disregarded the fact that existing laws included no religious or ethnic quotas, only national ones. Laughlin's report came out just a few days after the passenger ship *St. Louis*, filled with Jewish refugees, was not allowed to land on US soil. Many of those on board were taken back to Germany where they became victims of the holocaust.[37]

While it is important to acknowledge that unchallenged anti-Semitism in the US helped inspire and even shape the policies of Nazi Germany, no story of American anti-immigration sentiment would be complete without acknowledging the internment of Japanese citizens during World War II. Although Christian leaders may not have led the charge to put Japanese Americans into concentration-camp-type conditions, few raised any protests to this abhorrent policy.[38]

Following World War II, limited legal immigration coupled with a booming economy reduced the amount of national focus on immigration policy. In 1965, however, President Lyndon Johnson signed the Hart-Cellar Act, which effectively removed immigration quotas based on nationality and prioritized the family reunification and unique skills as rationales for allowing new people into the country.[39] More recently, however, the nation's attention has turned to undocumented or "illegal" immigrants who have either overstayed their work visas, crossed the border illegally, or come to the country as minors. President Ronald Reagan signed the Immigration and Control Act in 1986 that tightened border security and provided a pathway to citizenship for many undocumented immigrants already in the United States.[40]

Over the past few decades, the rhetoric and stereotyping of all immigrants, both documented and undocumented, has once again reached a fever pitch. In addition to talk radio pundits, Catholic-turned-Evangelical-Christian and former congressperson Tom Tancredo has helped lead the anti-immigration charge.[41] As many fight for comprehensive immigration reform that would provide a pathway to citizenship for the 12 million undocumented in the land, many churches and church leaders have once again responded with hate. Just a few years ago, Evangelical leader Jerry Falwell issued a strong call for leaders in Washington, DC, to take a strong stance against illegal immigrants:

We must get tough on illegal immigration and begin enforcing present laws throughout our nation.... The construction of a 2000-mile fence (which some estimate will cost $10 billion), across our southwest border, from San Diego to the Gulf of Mexico, guarded by enough of America's finest to stop the endless flow of scores of thousands of illegal aliens into this nation, must be the absolute commitment of our next champion. The bleeding must be stopped immediately.... Returning to adherence to our long-standing immigration laws is not an unreasonable demand. I realize I will be criticized by many for making this statement, but I am convinced we must halt the daily torrent of illegal immigrants who almost effortlessly enter our nation. I know that many of these people are simply seeking a better life, but countless numbers of criminals are entering our nation. Plus, contagious diseases that were virtually wiped out in America are resurfacing, primarily because of the flood of illegal immigration. It must stop.[42]

Falwell's attempt to link undocumented immigrants with crime and disease is consistent with earlier anti-immigrant perspectives of church leaders in this nation's history. The concern with crime, particularly along the Mexican border, led many Christians to support Arizona's controversial Senate Bill 1070, passed in 2010, which called for police officers to enforce immigration law and to demand proof of citizenship or legal papers from anyone who was suspected of being in the country without documents. While concerns about racial profiling led the bill to be put on hold by the courts, the presence of Christians in the US taking strong positions against immigrants remains.

In 2013, a bill offering significant reform to America's flawed immigration policy passed the US Senate with bipartisan support. Christian leaders joined with immigrant voices and organizations to help provide the momentum that made the Senate bill possible. Many Christian leaders, including the US Council of Catholic Bishops and a significant number of evangelical leaders, actively called for an immigration policy that keeps families together and offered an earned pathway to citizenship for eleven million undocumented immigrants living in the shadows.

As the Senate bill made its way to the US House of Representatives, a new organization emerged, calling itself "Evangelicals for Biblical Immigration." The group strongly opposed the Senate bill, suggesting that they understood the real biblical truth about immigration and that a pathway to citizenship was not biblical. The debate around how Scriptures written in an era before borders and modern nation states would respond to undocumented immigrants is legitimate and important. The Facebook page from the Evangelicals for Biblical Immigration suggests a much broader agenda, however. Posts by the group itself (not random postings by others commenting on their page) highlight far-right voices like Michelle Malkin while consistently stoking up fear by elevating a few anecdotes of the miniscule number of legal immigrants who participated in acts of terror. The site also supports a far-right-wing agenda that moves well beyond immigration, with posts critiquing the Affordable Care Act (Obamacare) and questions about the deaths at the US Embassy in Benghazi, Libya. Almost every mention of the Evangelical Immigration Table includes a dismissive and in essence nullifying connection to progressive billionaire George Soros, and another ridicules Rev. Jim Wallis by placing the "Rev." in quotation marks. Wallis is the founder of Sojourners, an evangelical magazine and organization that often advocates for more progressive social justice issues and concerns, leading to enmity with some on the more conservative side of the spectrum.[43] The tone of this group's rhetoric, not only with its protectionist agenda and embrace of American exceptionalism but also by linking evangelicals with a broad far-right ideology, adds to the long history of anti-immigrant rhetoric coming from the church.

Over the summer of 2013, Catholic representative Steve King from Iowa became one of the loudest anti-immigrant voices. In an August gathering in Virginia, King said the following about Latinos: "If you bring people from a violent civilization into a less-violent civilization, you're going to have more violence right? It's like pouring hot water into cold water, does it raise the temperature or not?"[44] Earlier he claimed that most undocumented youth are drug runners rather than people with the potential to positively contribute to the country: "For everyone who's a valedictorian, there's another hundred out there that weigh 130 pounds and they've got calves the size of cantaloupes because they're hauling 75 pounds of marijuana across the desert."[45] King's rhetoric, while widely condemned, demonstrates the spirit of nativism and anti-immigrant sentiment that has too often marked the American church's response to immigrants. Despite the romanticized image of Lady Liberty welcoming the teeming masses to America's shores, the real signs that have awaited many immigrants who have come to this land over the centuries are "Do Not Enter" and "No Trespassing." Sadly, the American Church has often led the charge to communicate disdain and even hatred for the immigrant in our land.

Theological Response

The power of theology is the power to generate a worldview that looks beyond the limitations of one's own culture, ethnicity, race, and place. The Christian capacity to see beyond one's own setting in order to engage God and others can be both its strength and its weakness. Christian theology raises the possibility that humanity is not limited by its bodily existence and can engage a transcendent imagination. At the same time, this capacity for transcendent vision can lead to a significant sense of arrogance and privilege by limited human beings. The capacity to connect with the divine can lead Christians to begin to believe they not only know what is best for the world, but that they are also preferred by God. When it comes to the church in the United States and its engagement with immigrants, hubris and arrogance have far too often ruled the day, leading white Protestants to exalt themselves over other ethnicities.

Theologian Willie Jennings asserts that theology is the "imaginative capacity to redefine the social."[46] Along the same lines, theologian Walter Brueggemann calls the church to a theology that engages the prophetic imagination. Brueggemann believes that "the task of prophetic ministry is to nurture, nourish, and evoke a consciousness and perception alternative to the consciousness and perception of the dominant culture around us."[47] The power of theology is the power to expand our imagination. William Cavanaugh provides a helpful definition of social imagination: "The imagination of a society is the sense of what is real and what is not; it includes a memory of how the society got where it is, a sense of who it is, and hopes and projects for the future.... [It] is the condition of possibility for the organization and signification of bodies in a society."[48]

The reality of a broken world, however, means that Christians often engaged in dysfunctional theological imagination. As Jennings asserts, "Christianity in the Western world lives and moves within a diseased social imagination."[49] When it comes to the engagement of Christians in the US with the plight of immigrants, this diseased imagination could be summarized as having two key expressions: a misunderstanding of Christian identity and the misuse of power in the context of Christian identity. The Christian contribution on the topic of immigration has been problematic, often leading to greater division and hostility rather than moving toward a greater unity.

The historical overview revealed that Christians often

engaged in harmful stereotypes about immigrant communities. Even Christians with missionary zeal for the conversion of those outside of the US would assume a sense of white superiority. Often, American Christians believed America to be the Promised Land for whites, to the exclusion of non-white immigrants. In other words, a warped Christian imagination that projected whiteness as normative, gave the power to white Christianity to project a defining negative image of the other. Christians attempted to seize the power to name another and assume power over the other. The resulting dysfunction yielded a Protestant agenda that often fostered an anti-immigrant agenda.

This diseased imagination springs from a misappropriation of the essential Christian doctrine of the *imago Dei*, or the belief that human beings are made in the image of God. This fundamental Christian belief means that humanity "bears and reflects the divine likeness among the inhabitants of the earth, because he[/she] is a spirit, an intelligent, voluntary agent."[50] The Christian understanding of the doctrine of the image of God means that "we could search the world over, but we could not find a man[/woman] so low, so degraded, or so far below the social, economic, and moral norms that we have established for ourselves that he[/she] had not been created in the image of God."[51]

The sin of the church was to take this meaningful doctrine that affirms the dignity of every human being and warp it to elevate one people group over another. The genesis of this sin involves reducing humanity's spiritual likeness to God to a physical likeness. Sin results when human beings attempt to take the place of God in creation. It is based upon the hubris of humanity to consider its own judgments of the world to be equal to God's judgments. Nativism, which elevates the native-born as more valuable than the immigrant, is a form of racism that elevates one people as the ultimate standard of reference to which other peoples should seek to emulate. In other words, white American Christians have made their own bodies the standard of reference in the determination of values and norms.

Anti-Chinese and anti-Japanese sentiment, for instance, was based upon the assumption that their otherness would be incompatible with American life and that the Asian "cannot be *Americanized*."[52] Matthew Jacobson presents Jacob Riis's account of life in Chinatown: "The inhabitants of Chinatown likewise seemed well beyond the moral reach of Christian civilization: 'All attempts to make an effective Christian of John Chinaman will remain abortive in this generation; of the next I have, if anything, less hope.'"[53]

The sin of the church was the inability to present a contrasting perspective to the prevailing notion of Anglo American, Protestant superiority.[54] Far too many Christian leaders and adherents assumed that a superior expression of God's image existed in the body of the white American, allowing the rejection of those who differ from the body image of the Anglo American. This belief reflects a fundamental violation of the image of God found in all people.

The elevation of one group as the standard by which all others should be judged ultimately undermines human community. A healthy Christian understanding of the image of God should result in a deeper sense of unity that moves beyond human division. Instead, a distortion of that doctrine furthers division and hostility. Theologian Emil Brunner states that since "God ... creates me in and for community with others ... the isolated individual is an abstraction ... the other, the others, are interwoven with my nature. I am not 'I' apart from the 'Thou.'"[55] The creation of the other alienates and separates the "I" from the "Thou" and yields a division of humanity that God did not intend. This state of division exacerbates the sense of otherness in American society. Correspondingly, there is a rejection and exclusion of the other, who are defined as those who differ from the standard of the white Christian American.

Christian Americans have been guilty of misapplying the doctrine of *imago Dei*, producing a broken community due to the belief in the inequality of human worth. The shared story of being made in the image of God should yield a sense of human unity. The diseased imagination has allowed for the dysfunctional belief that one people group holds a higher standing before God than another people group. "Western Christian intellectuals still imagine the world from the commanding heights."[56] The problem, however, with imagining the world from these heights is the fear and anxiety of falling from them and losing the privileges associated with that position. A sense of insecurity develops when privilege and command of theological control is challenged.

Part of the difficulty emerges from a misinterpretation of Genesis 1, which establishes that people are created in God's image, therefore they have dominion over the rest of creation. This authority, however, should be applied as the responsibility of human beings to properly care for creation. It is not license to rule over other human beings in the name of God. In the Hebrew Bible, there are frequent references to a covenant agreement between God and God's people that leads to the granting of land. The Bible seems to indicate a close connection between a people and their land. In fact, it is the Creator who is responsible for the establishment of a people upon the land. Still, the people do not ultimately own the land, God does. Humanity, therefore, cannot be understood in isolation. Human identity arises out of one's connection to the land and to the surrounding environment.

The formation of a people and the formation of a culture are not separated from the land and one's natural context. Given the importance of the connection of a people to the environment, the absence of that connection between the English colonists and the North American continent results in a growing insecurity within the white inhabitants. Since the land was improperly obtained, that land is tenuously held.[57] Ironically, one of the key American mediating narratives is the right to own property. It is one of the defining characteristics by which Americans can identify themselves as Americans — the ability to own the land. The American mythos of land ownership stands in contrast to a people that stewards the land that has been granted to them by God. Our insecurity regarding our rights to the land is a result of the elevation of land ownership on an economic level, without a deep understanding of the theological value of land.

Stuart Banner in *How the Indians Lost Their Land* explores the question of whether the English colonists viewed the Native Americans as the actual owners of North America. If the land rights of Native Americans were recognized, the colonists would have to purchase the land. Banner argues that there was a general understanding among the colonists that Native Americans owned the land. Even beginning with the baseline assumption that recognized "the Indians as owners of the whole continent," the land was believed to be "disproportionately large to the Indians' small numbers."[58] Therefore, "the principle of Indian land ownership was never recognized with unanimity. There were always some English colonists, and sometimes even some colonial governments, willing to take land from the Indians without paying for it. All laws are violated sometimes, and this one was violated more than most."[59]

The acquisition of Native lands, therefore, was often in violation of the colonists' own laws and revealed an unjust usurpation of land from the rightful owners. This usurpation was often accomplished under the guise of a political, social, spiritual, and moral superiority. Because this land was acquired under less than ideal and less than moral circumstances, there is an underlying insecurity of those whose possession of the land does not arise out of a theological justification. Therefore, when additional waves of immigrants arrived on these shores, the insecurity over the proper ownership of the land requires a theological justification simply to secure borders.

This deep-seated insecurity calls into question the dominant culture's rights to the land in the first place. For Christians, there should be the awareness that usurping native lands would be considered a notable sin in the eyes of God. The accompanying acts of genocide would also be a place of significant insecurity before God. Given this insecurity, would the current occupants of the land feel the fullness of anxiety and fear when the original owners of the land return? Would that anxiety extend toward any new people group that would arrive in North America? A lack of a prophetic imagination results in the need to preserve one's standing, however tenuous, as the masters and owners of the land. Despite what may be a false claim to that land, there is the fear of being brought down from a self-anointed space of superiority when the other is brought into the midst of them.

For Christians, the image of God finds its complete fulfillment in the person of Jesus. Colossians 1:15 states that "the Son is the image of the invisible God, the firstborn over all creation." Jesus is the ultimate expression of God's image. Central to understanding Jesus as the fulfillment of God's image is recognizing the Jewish identity of Jesus the Messiah. The tendency to separate Jesus the Christ from his Jewish Messianic identity results in an incomplete understanding of salvation. In other words, the inability to see Christian identity through the lens of the Jewish story yields the elevation of the Gentile identity in contrast to the biblical account.

The story of Ruth provides an alternative vision of the

relationship between God's chosen people and the Gentiles. The book of Ruth is the story of an immigrant grafted onto the tree of the chosen people. Her story becomes a part of the story of the Jews and reveals that God is a God of gracious inclusion. God is willing to include an outsider, a Gentile, one that is outside of the story of the chosen people, to become a key figure in the story of redemption. God is willing to include a Gentile into a story that does not belong to the Gentile. In the process of this gracious inclusion, Ruth, the Gentile, becomes a part of the greater blessing of God.

Ruth was a Moabite woman who had married into Naomi's Jewish family. When Naomi's husband, then subsequently her sons, die, Naomi journeys with her two daughters-in-law (Ruth and Orpah) back toward the land of Israel. While Orpah would eventually follow Naomi's admonition to return to Moab, Ruth insisted that "where you go I will go, and where you stay I will stay. Your people will be my people and your God my God" (Ruth 1:16). The Moabites were a people prohibited from approaching the holy sanctuary of God (Deuteronomy 23:3), which was reserved solely for God's people. But as the story unfolded, despite being an outsider, Ruth was accepted as one of the chosen people. In fact, she became an expression of God's grace grafted into the ancestry of King David and eventually of Jesus the Messiah.

For Ruth, immigration was her salvation. Her journey to a new land and her identification with her new home resulted in her encounter with God's salvation. Her geographic mobility led to her encounter with the promises of God through his people. In contrast, for the European colonists, movement toward the North American continent meant conquest rather than connection to the land. In fact, the land would be seen as being saved by the advent of the European presence in North

America. They achieved "salvation" via human effort rather than through the grace of God.

The story of Ruth as an immigrant foreshadows the story of Jesus as an immigrant. Jesus is one who journeys. His first journey was from the heavenly places to earth below. His incarnation proved to be the ultimate immigrant story. The narrative of Jesus reflects a journey from privilege to suffering. This journey needs to be understood in the context of Jesus' Jewish identity. Understanding Christian salvation requires understanding the great gulf that a Gentile crosses in order to be considered a part of God's chosen people. That journey requires an understanding of Jesus as the presence of the divine as well as the presence of the human. Jesus' human identity cannot be separated from his Jewish identity.

In the account of Ruth, we see that Gentiles are allowed to participate in the salvation offered to the Jews. In the same way, Gentiles are invited into the salvation story through the incarnation of Jesus. The fulfillment of God's promise through Jesus presupposes that God's plan for salvation does not change. God does not change his mind about offering his grace through the human venue and context of the Jews.[60] As David Novak explains, "If God broke his original promise to Israel . . . then how could the Church—as the branch grafted onto the tree—possibly believe God's ultimate promise to her?"[61] The understanding of the undeserved grace of God that anchors the Christian view of salvation should be consistent with God's grace at work among God's chosen people.[62] The Christian doctrine of grace should not be distanced from God's interaction of grace with the Jewish people.

The problematic aspect of this disconnect between God's acting of grace toward the Jewish people and the extension of grace toward the Gentiles has meant that Christianity could become disembodied from a particular context. Because God's grace no longer requires a human context, there was the successful act of expressing Christian faith from the perspective of the dominant power, namely European identity. As J. Kameron Carter states:

> The loss of a Jewish-inflected account—and thus a covenantal, nonracial account—of Christian identity cleared the way for whiteness to function as a replacement doctrine of creation. Hence, the world was re-created from the colonial conquests from the late fifteenth century forward in the image of white dominance, where "white" signifies not merely pigmentation but a regime of political and economic power for arranging ... the world.[63]

Carter finds that the severing of Christianity from its Jewish roots allows Christianity to become embedded in Western culture. "Behind the modern problem of race is the problem of how Christianity and Western civilization came to be thoroughly identified with each other, a problem linked to the severance of Christianity from its Jewish roots."[64] The Western Christian account of a Messiah stripped of his Jewishness results in a dysfunctional imagination. This dysfunctional imagination results in the elevation of white identity as the force for salvation in American society, above the salvation work of God.

The product of a failed Christian imagination is the lie of white American exceptionalism. The successful excising of the Jewish roots of Christianity now yields a dysfunctional Christianity divorced from her origins and wedded to a new cultural form. Christianity became embedded in Western, white cultural expression and could now be reduced to a white American form. As Carter explains, "Christology ... was problematically deployed to found the modern racial imagination."[65] The capitalistic and cultural triumph and the hegemony of whiteness meant that American society would feel the authority to define itself as the pinnacle of the created order. "Whiteness came to function as a substitute for the Christian doctrine of creation, thus producing a reality into which all else must enter."[66] With the theological elevation of whiteness as normative, the way was cleared to allow the definition of American culture from the perspective of white America.

The rise of the concept of American exceptionalism is a theological problem. Belief in exceptionalism is fundamentally related to how people view themselves in relationship to God. The sin of setting up one's own physical image as the ultimate ideal results in an exaggerated self-perception. This assumption of superiority allows the white Christian American to take a position of final authority over who has rights in the land. Taking this level of authority over the other arises out of a deep sense of insecurity of one's precarious position in the created order. To justify the taking of another's land, there has to be an assertion of one's own worth tied to one's success and accomplishments. It is a position achieved by the white American, rather than endowed by their Creator. Nativism is the assertion of one's own accomplishment and inflated self-perception in lieu of community and unity with the other.

This problem of nativism is exacerbated by the passivity of the Christian community. A dysfunctional Christian imagination is unwilling to protest against the dehumanization of the immigrant. The use of terms like "illegal immigrant" stands against the powerful story that all of humanity was made in the image of God. The inability of Christianity to stand against falsehood and speak truth to address a dysfunctional worldview is a failure of the Christian imagination.

Signs of Hope and a Prayer of Confession and Lament

Late January 2013, Christian Churches Together (CCT) gathered in Austin, Texas, for its seventh official Annual Meeting.

CCT represents the breadth of Christian denominations in the US, including: Historic Protestant, Catholic, Orthodox, Evangelical/Pentecostal, and Historic Black Church denominations. In subsequent years CCT focused on issues of poverty and racism. This year leaders of this diverse body focused on the need for broad reform of the US immigration system.

Over the course of four days, this coalition learned the history of immigration in the US, sought biblical counsel, watched films about life along America's southern border, and listened to the testimonies of "dreamers," undocumented domestic workers, and asylum-seekers. In the end the five families of the church in the United States reached consensus on a statement calling for just and humane immigration reform that includes an "earned path to citizenship."

Many statements have been issued by individual denominations and by particular arms of the American church. The US Conference of Catholic Bishops released a statement November 13, 2012. The Evangelical Immigration Table released a statement June 12, 2012. Likewise, individual historic Protestant denominations have released statements in the past. This is the first time that this broad band of the church has reached consensus on a single statement that calls for comprehensive immigration reform.

The CCT statement calls "people of faith, people of good will, elected officials in Congress and the president of the United States to work together to enact just and humane immigration reform legislation in 2013." A particular spiritual call for immigration reform, CCT reminds us: "While immigration is often viewed as an economic, social, or legal issue, it is ultimately a humanitarian and spiritual issue that directly impacts millions of unauthorized immigrants and the entire fabric of our society." It then goes on to demand "comprehensive reform now."

In one passage, the statement reflects on the significance of America's current moment in light of the January 1, 2013, celebration of the 150th anniversary of the Emancipation Proclamation:

> The timing of our statement on immigration is ever more poignant given that our country is celebrating the 150th anniversary of the Emancipation Proclamation. We are reminded that there are those in our nation whose forebears were brought here involuntarily through the unjust institution of slavery. There are also those who lived here long before others arrived who experienced the denial of their basic human rights. Each day in our congregations and communities, we bear witness to the effects of a system that continues this legacy of separation of families and the exploitation, abuse, and deaths of migrants. This suffering must end.

The statement continues: "Therefore, in our relentless effort to achieve a more perfect union, we urge our elected officials to enact immigration reform consistent with the following principles and policies ..." Over the next page the CCT statement outlines five principles to guide reform legislation:

- An earned path to citizenship for the 11 million people in the United States without authorization.
- The priority of family reunification in any immigration reform.
- Protecting the integrity of our borders and protecting due process for immigrants and their families.
- Improving refugee protection laws and asylum laws.
- Reviewing international economic policies to address the root causes of unauthorized immigration.

A press release issued by CCT explains that the statement will be followed by advocacy to members of Congress from the membership of denominations and groups represented at the Austin meeting. Within hours of issuing the CCT statement, the advocacy began. Representative denominations have begun to issue statements of their own in support of the CCT statement. Many have also committed to lead their own denominations to take the Evangelical Immigration Table's "I Was a Stranger Challenge," a grassroots initiative urging congregations to read forty biblical passages about immigration over forty days and ask their legislators to do the same.

We offer Psalm 60 as a lament prayed from the perspective of immigrants who have experienced great pain and suffering.

psalm 60

You have rejected us, God, and burst upon us;
*   you have been angry—now restore us!*
You have shaken the land and torn it open;
*   mend its fractures, for it is quaking.*
You have shown your people desperate times;
*   you have given us wine that makes us stagger.*
But for those who fear you, you have raised a banner
*   to be unfurled against the bow.*

Save us and help us with your right hand,
*   that those you love may be delivered.*
God has spoken from his sanctuary:
*   "In triumph I will parcel out Shechem*
*   and measure off the Valley of Sukkoth.*
Gilead is mine, and Manasseh is mine;
*   Ephraim is my helmet,*
*   Judah is my scepter.*
Moab is my washbasin,
*   on Edom I toss my sandal;*
*   over Philistia I shout in triumph."*

Who will bring me to the fortified city?
  Who will lead me to Edom?
Is it not you, God, you who have now rejected us
  and no longer go out with our armies?
Give us aid against the enemy,
  for human help is worthless.
With God we will gain the victory,
  and he will trample down our enemies.

CHAPTER 7

sins against jews and muslims

Historical Reflections

A common debate in many American churches is whether or not the United States flag should be displayed on the altar on Sunday morning. Many American Christians have strong feelings about the alignment of patriotism and their faith in Jesus. Many of these ideas are deeply rooted in the ideology embraced by the early American colonists that the New World provided the opportunity to establish a New Zion as a part of the manifestation of God's providential plan for the redemption of the world.

As Puritan colonists settled what was to become the New England coast, they viewed themselves as playing a particular role as "the chosen" in the masterpiece of God's will being manifested. These chosen people "were heirs to a covenantal promise and were entrusted with the task of building the Kingdom of God, the 'little American Israel.'" This became a "symbol of their spiritual and temporal labors" of the people of God with the goal of bringing about the New Jerusalem, "the ultimate cry of Protestant Christianity." As American colonists viewed themselves playing a unique role in God's plan for the world, they turned their eyes to the Holy Land as a source of inspiration and religious enthusiasm.[1]

As early as 1835, French historian Alexis de Tocqueville identified the assumptions behind American exceptionalism in the newly established nation of the United States. He noted that Americans adhered to the belief "that the then-fifty-year-old nation held a special place among nations, because it was a country of immigrants and the first modern democracy."[2]

Even as recently as September 2013, contemporary critics of the US, such as Russian President Vladimir Putin, have assaulted American exceptionalism.[3] Putin expressed blatant disapproval toward America for attributing equality and freedom to God's providential hand at work on behalf of the United States. The correlation of liberal democracy and the manifestation of God's will is a common thread throughout the history of the United States.

The Land of the Bible is a significant geographic place when it comes to understanding the manifestation of God's will. The Holy Land has long held both spiritual and material significance for Christians throughout American history. The Holy Land, as the birthplace of Jesus, has been associated with the kingdom of God. As Americans increasingly viewed the United States a "symbolic" kingdom of God, they also transferred their attention to concrete realities in the Holy Land. Historian Fuad Sha'ban writes: "The Orient [including the Middle East] became for many Americans the field of action for both the political and religious sides of Manifest Destiny."[4]

Manifest Destiny was the idea that European settlers were "destined" and ordained by God to move across the American continent. While many leading Americans rejected the notion, Manifest Destiny was the primary ideology used as the justification for western expansionism and the acquisition of new territories, including the land obtained from the Louisiana Purchase (1803), the annexation of Texas from Mexico (1845), and the Oregon Treaty (1846). Manifest Destiny had significant implications for the expansion of slavery and further devastation of the indigenous people already living on the territories conquered by the United States.

While Manifest Destiny was not purely a Christian belief and political practice, the notion was deeply rooted in ideas of American exceptionalism and the belief that the United States was unique among the nations in God's divine plan. Nonetheless, some of these early American assumptions continue to be carried out by beliefs and practices of contemporary Christians in the United States. Academic and historian Charles Marsh writes of this phenomenon: "Forgetting the difference between discipleship and patriotism, the God most Americans trust is a simulacrum of the holy and transcendent God, a reification of the American way of life."[5]

Adam Taylor, a leading American evangelical and former vice president of advocacy for the Christian development and humanitarian organization World Vision, writes: "But America is not a proxy for God. A belief that God favors American leadership devolves into hubris and a form of triumphalism. While our nation has been blessed with material riches, these blessings can't come at the expense of the rest of the world."[6]

This sentiment is shared by many conservative evangelicals, including Dr. Richard Land, former president of the Southern Baptist Convention's commission on Ethics and Religious Liberty. Land shares:

Ultimate allegiance belongs to God. But God is not an American. He may choose to bless America or judge America, but He is not an American. Many Americans worship Him, but He is not an American. And America's purposes are not necessarily God's purposes. We must never presume that America's policies serve God's purposes. The besetting sin of conservatives is to merge God and country as if they are virtually inseparable.[7]

Taylor and Land's reminder to contemporary American Christians is a challenge to the assumptions of American exceptionalism. God's purposes and plan are greater than any one nation state and should be viewed in light of his greater purposes for the world.

One of the greatest negative consequences of American exceptionalism is the historic assumption that whites, or individuals who might most readily be associated with the American norm, are more included and welcomed into the privileges society has to offer. From early in the history of the United States, race and social dissimilarities served as differentiating factors that further isolated the indigenous Native American community and enslaved blacks and other communities of color. Race, however, was not the only category of discrimination. Religion, more specifically adherence to the social norm of Christianity, also significantly contributed to whether people would be welcomed into mainstream society. The Jewish community in America is one such community that Christians have treated with distrust, negative stereotypes, and isolation. With this in mind, it is important to look more deeply at the historic treatment of the Jewish people by American Christians.

Anti-Semitism, as defined by many dictionaries, refers to discrimination or hostility toward Jews. Semites are descendants of Shem, the son of Noah. The term Semite includes Jews and Near Eastern groups such as Arabs, Ethiopians, Hebrews, and other Semitic-speaking peoples. Nonetheless, the term anti-Semitism in contemporary American society most commonly refers to discrimination and ill treatment toward Jewish people. Alan Dershowitz, lawyer and political commentator, writes in *The Case for Israel*, "A good working definition of anti-Semitism is taking a trait or an action that is widespread, if not universal, and blaming *only* the Jews for it."[8]

Historic and contemporary anti-Semitism is a global phenomenon. The Nazi Holocaust that resulted in the extermination of more than six million Jews is the most significant expression of contemporary anti-Semitism, but unfortunately that was not the only expression of hatred toward Jews at that time. There were others, some of which were associated with fundamental assumptions of some prominent Christian theologies and ideologies.[9] Ethicist Richard Land notes that "three of the most prominent Protestant scholars of the twentieth century ... became enmeshed with the Nazi movement and to varying degrees became spokesmen for the Nazi cause: Paul Althaus (1888 – 1966), Emanuel Hirsch (1888 – 1972), and the renowned Gerhard Kittel (1888 – 1948), whose *Theological Dictionary of the New Testament* is still in use as one of the most important works of biblical scholarship of the twentieth century."[10]

Anti-Semitism on the American Christian scene was expressed through views and interpretations of early nineteenth-century Protestant missionaries. Levi Parsons, American Christian Missionary, espoused a commonly held view that Jews were "degenerate children" whose hands were "imbued in the blood of the Son of God."[11] This was a classic form of anti-Semitism where the Jewish people were most recognized as the murderers of Jesus Christ on the cross. While the theological tenants of dispensationalism were on the rise in the late nineteenth century, many conservative and fundamentalist Christians were also committed to anti-Semitic practices.

Fundamentalists adopted a negative view of Jews, considering them to be "Christ-killers," and most fundamentalists were opposed to the Zionist enterprise of returning Palestine to the Jewish people as a homeland.[12]

In the 1940s, in the midst of the Nazi Holocaust, Jewish refugees were denied entry to countries around the world based on such anti-Semitic sentiments. The United States, while less anti-Semitic than its European counterparts, significantly limited its immigration to Jewish refugees fleeing Nazi Germany. Many argue that international support, including that coming from the conservative Christian community in the United States, supported Jewish establishment of Palestine because of anti-Semitism. European nations and countries did not want Jewish refugees flocking to their borders and thus determined that the establishment of the nation-state of Israel should be pursued as an alternative solution to the Jewish refugee crisis.

In 1966, Charles Glock, a University of California professor and sociologist of religion, conducted the first-ever work (with Rodney Stark of the University of Washington) to determine whether empirical, quantitative data exists that show that particular Christian theologies and practices support anti-Semitism.[13] In reference to the Glock-Stark Anti-Semitism Survey, the leading Protestant liberal periodical *The Christian Century* concluded: "In late 1959 and early 1960, a burst of anti-Semitism in Europe and the United States rudely awakened us to the fact that the centuries of hatred of the Jews had not been ended with the Third Reich."[14] Rather, theological anti-Semitism in the US continued well into the mid-twentieth century and beyond.

American Christian perspectives toward the establishment of the modern nation-state of Israel are complex. Many US Christians, particularly in light of the military success of Israel during the Six Day War in 1967, view the Jewish return to their historic homeland as prophetic fulfillment. These conservative Christians, sometimes called Christian Zionists, believe the return of Christ will be precipitated by Jewish return to the land in unbelief. Other Christian groups adopt replacement theology, which asserts that the Christian church supersedes, or replaces, the Jewish people in God's divine plan. Replacement theologians believe the church inherits the promises that God made to the Jewish people. Alan Dershowitz, heavily critical of replacement theology, argues that it is a type of "theological anti-Semitism."[15] He sees replacement theology as a threat to the fundamentals of Jewish identity.

Aside from these perspectives, it is important to note that many Christians believe Jews require conversion, just like anyone else, in order to inherit the kingdom of heaven. So some Christians pursue the evangelization of Jews as a means of loving them into the kingdom.

In the twenty-first century, some progress has been made in Christian-Jewish dialogue in the US. There has been a theological shift away from the belief that Jews are responsible for Christ's death on the cross. Nonetheless, anti-Semitism within the American Christian community must continue to be addressed. Tony Maalouf, theologian and author of *Arabs in the Shadow of Israel*, while acknowledging anti-Jewish anti-Semitism encourages Christians to be on their guard against other kinds of prejudices:

> Anti-Semitism was an ugly phenomenon that engendered many atrocities against the Jews over many centuries in Europe. It desperately needed to be addressed. Today the world may be unconsciously replacing anti-Semitism with a different kind of racial favoritism—anti-Arabism. This only magnifies the problem and establishes a situation that will merely pass on the problems to the next generation.[16]

Christians in America should be similarly concerned with

the growing anti-Arab sentiment present in social media out-
lets, news programs, and mainstream society. M. J. Rosenberg,
a Jewish senior foreign-policy fellow at Media Matters Action
Network, is deeply concerned that American society is unfairly
characterizing the entire Muslim community as radicalized terrorists and extremists. *Islamophobia* is the term that has been
coined to refer to negative assumptions, racism, and fear toward
Muslims. Since the attacks against the United States on September 11, 2001, there has been increasing distrust and prejudice against people who practice Islam.

Arabs and Muslims were not always viewed as the enemy by
American Christians. Attention toward the Arab world by US
Christians has been deeply motivated by evangelistic aspira-
tions and missionary attentiveness. Formal American affairs in
the Arab world began with the establishment of the American
Oriental Society in 1842.[17] The rise of Christian missionaries
to the Arab world began in the second half of the nineteenth
century when Americans felt it their call and duty to be faithful servants of God's kingdom. According to Sha'ban, they
believed the "future of the Arab World and the fate of its people
was not only a privilege, but an obligation for the missionary,
the politician, and the layman."[18] Americans carried out their
exceptionalist assumptions through a sort of theological imperialism, which included a religious zeal to "fuel the vision of
Zion" and was expressed in "missionary concern for the 'lost'
Muslim souls."[19]

Missionary efforts and zeal for conversion are legitimate
aims for evangelical Christians who believe Christ's kingdom is
only available to those who profess faith. But it is important to
understand how people of other religious persuasions interpret
and experience Christian efforts of evangelism. In addition,
evangelistic efforts were often not only about sharing the Gospel message but were distorted by other exceptionalist notions

that resulted in the abuse and isolation of the receiving population. The zeal of Christian evangelism was pursued at all costs even when it resulted in causing harm to those being converted. As recently as 2009, an executive of a leading Christian development organization used language of "conquering the Middle East" for Christ just the way Joshua and Caleb looked to the hilltops that had not yet been won for God's glory.

Twentieth-century American views toward Islam have become increasingly anti-Islamic. Academic Ralph Braibanti of Duke University asserts that Islamophobia is a growing trend present in conservative American Christian circles.[20] He asserts three primary reasons for this growing prejudice: (1) the Arab-Israeli conflict; (2) the rise of Arab fundamentalism and militancy; and (3) the rise of US visibility and political power of evangelical fundamentalist Protestant Christians who emphasize the Hebraic law and biblical inerrancy.[21] Braibanti sees a correlation between Christians who have conservative interpretations of the Scriptures and the belief that Muslims are evil and want to take over the world for the sake of a cause counter to Christianity.

In addition to the negative realities of historic Palestinian and Arab terrorism surrounding the Arab-Israeli conflict, Braibanti claims that the American portrayal of the Arab-Israeli conflict "results in massive campaigns of disinformation and vituperation damaging to Islam and to the Arab image."[22] The universal application and distortion of the Islamic notion of *jihad* has increased the misperception held by many Americans that all Muslims are terrorists who desire to destroy infidels who do not similarly adhere to their religious beliefs. In addition, Braibanti asserts Christian fundamentalists such as Jerry Falwell "powerfully reinforce earlier misconceptions by linking Judaism and Christianity and, at least by implication, isolating Islam as the enemy of both."[23] More specifically, Braibanti cites "the millenarian attitude, embedded in Old Testament prophesy linked with the quest for a New World Zion," as expressed in the naming of places such as "Salem, Sinai, Nazareth, Providence, New Jerusalem ... and similar New World communities," is identified as the distorting force of American Christian perceptions toward Muslims.[24]

In 2010, Terry Jones, an evangelical pastor from Gainesville, Florida, captured the attention of the world when he announced his plan to burn the Islamic holy book, the Qur'an. Many would claim Jones an outlier to American Christianity, but his actions significantly affected the views of the Arab world toward Americans. With passionate conviction, which Jones claimed was compelled by his Christian faith, he professed he had the right to burn the book because it was "full of lies."[25] He declared that "Islam is of the devil" and, thus, must be exposed.

Ron McNeil, a Florida candidate for Congress who espoused similar beliefs, told a group of high school and middle school students that Islam's goal is to "destroy our way of life ... [thus] it is our place as Christians to stand up for the word of God and what the Bible says."[26] The Qur'an-burning issue died down a bit when Pastor Jones responded to the pleas of world leaders and agreed not to act out his initial threat. The following spring, however, he hosted a small ceremony with about thirty people present and burned a Qur'an in order to draw the attention of the world to the evils of Islam. The act was condemned by world leaders and Muslims alike and provoked deadly protests throughout the Muslim world. In Mazar-I-Sharif, Afghanistan, an angry mob, incited by three Islamic mullahs, killed twelve people — seven United Nations workers and five Afghans.[27]

Jones's burning of the Qur'an may be discredited by many as an extremist act by one American Christian. But it is critical for Christians to ask whether some of Jones's core assumptions are more broadly spread throughout American Christian communities. Regardless of one's theological beliefs toward Islam, the Christian community must learn to respect and acknowledge people of different cultural backgrounds, faiths, and religions. Just as theological beliefs negatively impact Judeo-Christian relations through the expression of anti-Semitism, American Christians must be similarly concerned that we do not act out of hatred, distrust, and prejudice toward men and women who practice Islam.

Theological Reflections

On July 21, 1656, Elizabeth Key Grinstead, a woman of African and English descent, sued for her freedom on the basis that her father was an Englishman and therefore, according to English law, she was an English citizen and could not be enslaved. In addition, she had been baptized as a Christian. Grinstead became the first woman of African descent in the colonies to sue for her freedom and win. According to writer Taunya Lovell Banks, Christian status did not ensure release from slave status, but it did reinforce Key's status as an English citizen.[28] Yet Banks sites other claims by historian Edmond Morgan, author of *American Slavery, American Freedom: The Ordeal of Colonial Virginia* (1975), who believed that "before 1660 it was assumed that Christianity and slavery were incompatible." She goes on to say "he admits that 'in Virginia [there always had been] a rough congruity of Christianity, whiteness, and freedom and of heathenism, non-whiteness, and slavery." In the same footnote, Banks explains, "Morgan cites a 1662 General Assembly order to release a Powhatan Indian enslaved for life who was 'speaking perfectly the English tongue and desiring baptism.'"[29]

In 1667, eleven years after the Grinstead case, five years after the Powhatan Indian case, and two months after a black slave named Fernando lost his suit for freedom because the papers he presented to prove his claim of Christian birth were written in Spanish or Portuguese (not English) — Virginia's General Assembly enacted a law that declared that Christian baptism would not, heretofore, change the slave status of the converted.[30]

So why, in a chapter about anti-Semitism and Islamophobia, do we mention colonial slavery? Because these cases reveal something deeper; they show a fundamental thought pattern, with roots in colonial America, that has woven its way through history and into American Christian thought into the twentieth and twenty-first centuries. We are talking about the fundamental belief that human dignity is not inherent, that it is only conferred upon conversion.

Leo Max Frank was part owner of a pencil factory in Atlanta, Georgia. On April 16, 1913, one of his workers, thirteen-year-old Mary Phagan, picked up her paycheck and was murdered soon afterward. Frank was accused, charged, tried, and convicted of Phagan's murder later that year. His sentence was death by hanging. Multiple appeals and protests of Frank's conviction and sentence were mounted across the country over the next two years. Under outside pressure, Georgia governor John M. Slaton commuted the sentence from death to life imprisonment only days before Frank's scheduled execution. When news of Slaton's intervention got out national guardsmen were called in to guard Slaton's home from the mobs that marched outside screaming: "We want John M. Slaton, King of the Jews and traitor Governor of Georgia!" On August 16, 1915, twenty-five men kidnapped Frank from his jail cell in Milledgeville, Georgia, drove him 118 miles to Marietta, and lynched him there. Among the assailants was a Christian pastor.[31]

In 1986, new evidence cleared Frank, and he was posthumously pardoned. The evidence pointed to Jim Conley, a janitor who worked in the factory and falsely accused Frank of the murder. Leo Frank is the only Jewish man ever to have been lynched in the United States. While the extreme violence perpetrated against him stands as an anomaly in the Jewish American experience, the particulars of the churches' responses offer insight into the mindset of Christian denominations and leaders of the time.

According to Robert Seitz Frey, author of the *Georgia Historical Quarterly*'s 1987 article, "Christian Responses to the Trial and Lynching of Leo Frank," most Christian periodicals did not cover Frank's case until after the lynching. They didn't cover the massive protests of his conviction or sentence. With one exception, they didn't cover the commutation of his sentence. The exception was a weekly Mennonite periodical that covered Slaton's commutation but made no mention of the lynching in all of its weekly issues that year. A few publications mentioned Frank's Jewish heritage and the anti-Jewish sentiment of the times, but most spoke of Frank in neutral terms. Never, though, did the publications give anything beyond the most basic identifying facts about the man; none of the kinds of descriptors that humanize one's subject.

None, that is, except the *Northern Christian Advocate*, who interviewed Frank's mother asking if she could forgive her son's assailants. She said that perhaps one day she "will be able to quote Leo's favorite passage from the Scriptures. It was: 'Father, forgive them, for they know not what they do.'"[32] Frey explains: "The *Advocate* editorialized: 'If this be as reported, it beautifully illustrates the influence of Jesus upon his brethren after the flesh.'"[33] Frank was humanized by the *Advocate* by revealing Jesus' influence upon him.

In his book, *The Cross and the Lynching Tree*, James H. Cone explains, "Even prominent religious scholars in the North, like the highly regarded Swiss-born church historian Philip Schaff of Union Theological Seminary in New York (1870–93), believed that 'the Anglo-Saxon and Anglo-American, of all modern races, possess the strongest natural character and the one best fitted for universal dominion.'"[34] To be sure, Schaff does say exactly that in his 1854 treatise, "America: A Sketch of the Political, Social, and Religious Character of the United States of North America," written eleven years before the American Civil War.[35] And he goes further.

Schaff explains the kind of dominion he speaks of is not one of despotism, but the kind that sets his subjects free. "In them—and this is the secret of their national greatness and importance—the impulse towards freedom and the sense of law and order are inseparably united, and both rest on a moral basis." Schaff continues, "Conscience and the sense of duty are very strongly marked in them, and I doubt whether the moral influence of Christianity and of Protestantism has more deeply and widely affected any nation, than it has the Anglo-Saxon."[36]

In Genesis 1:26–27, dominion is conferred upon humanity—all humanity. Dominion is often a misunderstood word. As discussed earlier, in the cultural context it would have meant something close to "steward." In modern terms, we might think of it as "human agency," the ability to make decisions that impact one's world. Humanity was given dominion over most of the rest of creation; over the seas and all the creatures in them, over the land and all the other creatures that walked the land, and over the birds of the sky. In fact, the command to exercise dominion is inextricably linked in the text to what it means to be human. In the same breath God says let us make humans in our image and let them have dominion. What separates humanity from the rest of creation is the very fact that we are made in the image of God and commanded to exercise dominion.

So what does it reveal that throughout early American

history, theologians, politicians, clergy, and journalists alike affirmed white Anglo-Saxon Protestants' exclusive ability, capacity, and even natural "fittedness" to exercise dominion? It reveals a deep-seated belief in the American psyche about what it means to be human: it is to be white, Anglo-Saxon, and Protestant. This is sin.

One does not have to convert to become human according to Scripture. One is born human, born with the image of God imprinted on one's soul. Every single human being on the face of the earth—from Timbuktu to Time Square, from the halls of the Church of England to the halls of Willow Creek Church, from the synagogues of Israel to the mosques of Baghdad, from the Hindu temples of India to the Buddhist temples in China—every single person on earth is made in the image of God. Therefore, all else being equal, every single person possesses the inherent ability, capacity, and "fittedness" to exercise dominion. It is sin to believe otherwise, and that sin is all the more destructive when such beliefs are put into practice.

The six-hour documentary, "The Jewish Americans," produced by David Gruben and broadcast on PBS in 2007, features a segment about discrimination against Jewish Americans in the workplace and public square. The segment begins, "Anti-Semitism in America was mostly a matter of custom, tradition, and gentleman's agreements, rather than statute, but it excluded Jews from fully participating in American life." Supreme Court Justice Ruth Bader Ginsburg remembers her first experience of anti-Semitism. She was on a trip with her parents. As they drove along a country road she saw a bed and breakfast with a sign in front. It read, "No dogs or Jews allowed." She explains that she had never seen a sign like that before. The look in her eyes as she recalls the moment says it all. Staring into the past with eyes that seem to get it for the first time; they think she is inhuman, she says, "That was obviously ... unsettling."[37]

Bernie Marcus, co-founder of Home Depot and founder of the Marcus Foundation, explains in the same segment that at the time it was nearly impossible to get a job at any major corporation if you were a Jew. And, in fact, the phrase "Christians Only" was used in many newspaper help wanted and personal ads in the early part of the twentieth century.

Hailed as one of the great innovators and industrial leaders in American history, Henry Ford, a nominal Episcopalian, was also a strident anti-Semite. His Michigan-based publishing house, the Dearborn Publishing Company, published a series of articles denigrating the "The International Jew." The articles were eventually collected into four volumes and titled *The International Jew: The World's Foremost Problem* (1920–22). In 1998, the *Washington Post* reported that a class-action suit had been filed against the Ford Motor Company by survivors of the Holocaust because direct connections had been made between the Ford Motor Company and Hitler's Third Reich. The Post reported:

> When the US Army liberated the Ford plants in Cologne and Berlin, they found destitute foreign workers confined behind barbed wire and company documents extolling the "genius of the Fuehrer," according to reports filed by soldiers at the scene. A US Army report by investigator Henry Schneider dated Sept. 5, 1945, accused the German branch of Ford of serving as "an arsenal of Nazism, at least for military vehicles" with the "consent" of the parent company in Dearborn.[38]

Most reports say Ford's Christian faith was not a driving force in his life. But perhaps it was his "thin faith," as Miroslav Volf puts it, that laid the groundwork for a soul capable of dehumanizing others in thought and deed.

In *A Public Faith*, Volf argues that "The cure against Christian violence is not less of the Christian faith, but, in a carefully qualified sense, *more* of the Christian faith."[39] Volf explains:

"'Thin' but zealous practice of the Christian faith is likely to foster violence; 'thick' and committed practices will help generate and sustain a culture of peace."[40] This thin faith is demonstrated by the rise of Islamophobia within portions of the American church after the terrorist attacks on September 11, 2001.

For example, Terry Jones, an evangelical pastor from Gainesville, Florida, demonstrated arguably "thin" Christian faith and practice when he burned the Qur'an. After all, when did Jesus burn a sacred Roman or Samaritan or Syrophoenician text of any of the people he visited with in his journeys? He didn't. Why? Because his goal was not to conquer, coerce, or shame the other into acceptance of his theological dominance. No. Christ's goal was to restore and repair all the relationships that God declared *tobe mehode*, "very good," in Genesis 1— all the relationships that were destroyed in Genesis 3. Christ did not try to defeat those who called him "enemy" or "other." Rather, he talked with them (John 3 and 4), he healed them (Luke 7), he reasoned with them and challenged them (Matthew 23), and he spread his arms wide and became obedient to death, even death on a cross for them (Matthew 27, Mark 15, Luke 23, John 19). And he prayed the prayer that Leo Max Frank reportedly loved: "Father, forgive them, for they know not what they do." With that prayer Jesus laid the foundation for what Volf calls "thick" Christianity—the kind of Christian faith that embraces one's enemies.

There have been plenty of examples of thin Christianity since 9/11. Christians and non-Christians alike called upon the City of New York to block the Park51 mosque and interfaith center from being built blocks from the site of the World Trade Center. As of August 2013, seven states—most with high populations of people who self-identify as Christian—have outlawed the use of Sharia Law in their court systems.[41] The first amendment to the Constitution of the United States outlaws the establishment of any one religious standard in any branch of government. So, it is not only a useless act to pass legislation banning one religion's texts from being used in the courtroom, it is also an aggressive act of social, cultural, and religious exclusion of one people group from society.

In each of these examples, the humanity of "the other" is lost, discounted, or simply not acknowledged. Rather, the Muslim is cast in the same light that Henry Ford cast the Jews—as less than human enemies seeking to take over America and destroy our way of life.

At the heart of it all is the deeply seated theological belief that humanity is conferred upon humans only after conversion. People's humanity is not recognized or acknowledged until they are Christians. Then, and only then, are they on equal ground. Until then, they are suspect at best; and they are inhuman enemies at worst.

Perhaps at the heart of some American Christians' dehumanization of non-Christians is a triumphal understanding of the Christian faith itself. Paul uses the language of war in his final exhortation to the Ephesians (6:10–20), calling them to put on the whole armor of God. He talks of breastplates and belts, shields, helmets, and swords. But it is worth noting that Paul launches the section with this frame: "Be strong in the Lord and in the strength of his power." The strength that Paul calls the Ephesians to adopt is not located in any actual practice of violence. On the contrary, Paul calls believers to recognize that there are spiritual powers that seek to do violence against them. He calls them to stand strong and fight, but to fight with the weapons of nonviolence: truth, righteousness (in the Greek, more accurately translated "justice" or "equity"), peace, faith, salvation, the Spirit, and the Word of God.

Thin faith mistakes Paul's charge as an affirmation of war

and violence. War creates an *us* versus *them* framework that leads to the dehumanization of the other and an unexamined posturing of the self as good, right, "fittest," and most human. This is natural. It is simply the default mode of war. Another fact of war is that there will be casualties. Perhaps the greatest casualty of this warlike attitude within the American church is its own witness. The witness of the church has been decimated. Restoration of the witness of the church to the Islamic and Jewish communities will require repentance. We must repent of our thin Christianity. We must repent of our failure to recognize the image of God in our Jewish and Muslim neighbors. We must repent of the ways we have hindered Jewish and Muslim citizens from exercising equal dominion within the fabric of American society. And we must repent of the subtle and not-so-subtle ways we have failed to recognize and affirm the human dignity of every man, woman, and child doing their prayers in mosques and synagogues across the nation and the world.

Signs of Hope and a Prayer of Confession and Lament

The September 11, 2011, "On Faith" section of the *Washington Post* included a letter from Pastor Aaron Graham of the District Church titled, "Letter from a Young Evangelical to the Muslim World." On the tenth anniversary of 9/11, Graham states: "The purpose of this letter is to ask for forgiveness and help clarify a common misunderstanding." After acknowledging that the spirit of revenge and vengeance has marked America's response to 9/11, the young pastor adopts a spirit of humility:

> The Bible talks a lot about fools. Fools are people who believe that the problem is always rooted in someone else. Ironically many fools are also very religious. Fools believe that if others would only change, the world would be a better place. The big problem with

fools is they do not own their part of the problem. They do not confess how their own sins may be contributing to the evil and injustice in the world. Many of us Christians in America have been fools. We have not taken Jesus's command seriously to take the plank out of our own eye so we can see the speck in our neighbor's eye. Too often we have associated all Muslims with violence and hatred. In doing so we have not modeled the way of Christ.

Graham ends his open letter with a call to action rooted in repentance and transformation:

On Sunday, the 10th anniversary of 9/11, our new church is taking up an offering for famine relief in the Horn of Africa. For us, this is a small act of reconciliation. A small but important way for us to say to the Muslim world that we are sorry for the ways we have portrayed you over the last 10 years. We want to make things right. Let's work together to make this world a safer, more just and peaceful place for everyone.

a prayer exercise

Reflection Prayer

Close your eyes and imagine a man or a woman. What is his first name? What is her last name? Where was she born? Where does he live now? How old is she? How much schooling has she achieved? What are his parents' jobs? Do they work in non-profit? Are they doctors, lawyers, or engineers? Are they educators, writers, or entertainers? Are they faith leaders? Do they own a restaurant or small business? Do they work in a restaurant or small business?

What is the funniest joke she knows? Who told him this joke?

What are her dreams for her life? What are his dreams for his family? What are his dreams for his community?

What are her dreams for our country?
What are God's dreams for her life? What are God's
dreams for his family? What are God's dreams for his
community? What are God's dreams for her country?
Now imagine this man or woman praying.
Now imagine them praying in a mosque or a synagogue.
Does God know her name?
Does God hear his cries?
Does God care about their dreams and family and
community and country?
Now open your eyes.
The answer is yes. Acts 10:1–35 reveals that God knows
their names. God hears their cries. God cares about
their dreams, their families, their communities, and
their country.

Listening Prayer
Be silent.
Plant both feet on the floor.
Breathe.
Listen to God's words to you about the real people whose
cries God hears every day … people who cry out in
every corner of the world; whether that corner is
peppered with steeples, temples, mosques, or synagogues.
Listen to God's heart for them.
Listen … Can you hear their cries?

Breath Prayer
When you're ready, breathe in deep.
As you breathe out, say "Forgive us."

conclusion

the cry of the church to the world should be "Forgive Us."
This book attempts to present the historical and theological reasons why confession is an absolute essential aspect of the witness of the church. At a time when the American church struggles with finding its place in the world and struggles with asserting its identity, could the church be known as the community that models confession, repentance, and the seeking of forgiveness? At this moment in history, the American church is often ridiculed or portrayed as unforgiving and ungracious. Could the church offer a counter-narrative, not of defensiveness or derision, but of an authentic confession and genuine reconciliation? By examining seven different areas where the church has committed sin, we ask the church to consider the spiritual power and the theological integrity of a church that seeks forgiveness for those sins.

Our Scriptures testify to the necessity of confession. Confession is central to the Christian faith. The importance of confession arises from the Christian view of sin. Sin is a reality and must be taken seriously. Evangelicals consistently begin our gospel presentation with the centrality of sin to the human experience. American evangelicals often assert that the beginning of the work of God's forgiveness is the recognition of our need for God because of human sinfulness.

The reality of sin points toward the necessity of grace. We experience the power of forgiveness and the joy of God's grace through the acknowledgment of our sin. In other words, we know amazing grace because we are aware of the depth of sin. Confession leads to grace. It is antithetical to the gospel when we do not confess all forms of sin—both individual and corporate. The reason evangelicals can claim to be followers of Jesus is because there has been an acknowledgement of sin and the seeking of God's grace through Jesus Christ that leads to the forgiveness of sin.

But in our corporate life, we spend a significant amount of time trying to deny our sin. We spend much of our time addressing the sins of others, while minimizing our own. We are willing to embrace the grace of God, but we do not often acknowledge the holiness of God, because we fail to confess how far we as a church have fallen short and continue to fall short of the glory of God. Our captivity to the hyper-individualism of Western culture may lead us to acknowledge that individual Christians have acted in an unworthy manner, but it often does not lead us to recognize our own complicity in corporate sinfulness.

Many may read the stories offered in this book and, as a result, focus on the individual failings of Christian leaders or key figures. It would be easy to blame the racists and sexists in the Christian community and distance ourselves from them. But we must begin to see the corporate responsibility that the church holds in our presentation to the world. How do we contribute and perpetuate the public wrongdoing of Christians through our silence and passivity?

For example, if a Christian is in a small group gathering and hears a racial slur or a racist remark, is that Christian guilty of offering implicit support for the statement simply by remaining silent? While that person may not have made the remark, he or she contributes to the hostile environment by not responding. By not offering the necessary counter-narrative, we end up endorsing a passive acceptance of the status quo. We affirm a toxic point of view in society because we choose to remain silent in the face of a sinful action.

In the same way, when an individual Christian, such as a Christian leader or public figure, presents a sinful point of view that claims to be Christian, other Christians, by remaining silent, affirm that public statement. All too often, Christians do not offer a contrasting perspective or a counter-narrative to sinful actions by other Christians in the public arena. We sin through our passive acceptance of the status quo.

The church, therefore, has the responsibility to offer a perspective that counters that dysfunctional representation. This book attempts to acknowledge the many places in our nation's history, as well as in contemporary Christianity, that have presented a sinful face to the world. In recognizing past and current sins, we, as people who uphold the tenets of Scripture, have no choice but to offer up confession on behalf of the church.

Even after the first step of acknowledging our sin (which alone is a significant challenge and an area of weakness for the American church), we often do not know how to actually confess or seek forgiveness. Even in small matters we are miserable at confessing. How are we expected to be effective at confession in larger matters? For example, a prominent Christian leader posted a social media entry that deeply offended many people. The intention was not to offend, but an offense had occurred. Initially, the pastor was defensive, claiming that it was meant to be a joke and that people should get over the offense. The initial denial of sin occurred. As the outcry continued, the pastor relented, removed the offensive image, and offered an apology. But even the apology focused on the fragility of those that were offended by offering pastoral care, and the apology began with the phrase "If you were offended . . ."

An offense had occurred. Many had articulated the deep nature of the wound. There was an action to undo the offense, but there was no clear articulation of sorrow, repentance, and confession. There have been too many instances of Christians (who should embrace the language of confession because it is so central to our theological framework) offering up halfhearted, poorly stated, soft-pedaled, self-serving "apologies." Our apologies are not confessions, they are excuses.

The evangelical church must more deeply develop the discipline of confession. We do not confess regularly, so when it comes time to confess, we don't do it very well. The Catholic Church may provide some direction for evangelicals in how to engage the practice of confession. Catholics often practice it as a regular rite in a specified location in each church building. Confession is a natural and regular part of Catholic Church life. Evangelicals, however, leave little room for confession, either as part of their individual lives or as part of their corporate life of worship.

The absence of confession in the American church is linked to the absence of lament. The church moves too quickly to praise and often skips over lament, which requires staying in the place of brokenness brought about by sin. It requires the recognition of human sinfulness. The church often allows our congregations either to ignore lament altogether or to move as quickly as possible past confession and lament toward praise and celebration. They treat confession as merely a stepping stone.

The absence of true confession reveals the church's cultural captivity to American triumphalism and exceptionalism. If the American church is, like the country itself, exceptional and destined for triumph, then there is no need to confess the sins of the past, because the end goal of elevating the American church justifies the sinful actions that lead to that triumph. Confession requires a deep humility that recognizes human sinfulness in light of God's holiness. American triumphalism and exceptionalism also need to be confessed in order to recognize the corporate sins of the American church.

Jesus is the hope of the world. Therefore, what we offer to the world as Christ's body on earth should reflect the grace and mercy of our Savior. By offering confession, we reflect the humility of Christ, which reflects the hope of salvation. Our faith has been compromised. When Christian pastors, leaders, and communities fail to live out God's redemptive plan for the world, our sin causes brokenness and pain. We should lament over this brokenness. And yet, because of God's grace, this is not the end of the story! When the community of believers acknowledges the error of its ways and repents, the love of Christ enters in.

Pastor Keith Stewart and his congregation have experienced this redemption firsthand. Stewart founded Springcreek Church in Garland, Texas, and has served the church community for twenty-three years. He tells a story of how his life, and the life of the church, was profoundly changed in 2006 after a visit to Kenya with World Vision. "I went to Africa thinking I was going to save them," he explains, "when God was really bringing Africa into my life to save me."

During Stewart's visit, he was devastated by the things he saw and experienced: "We were going into a slum called Soweto, a community that sprang up on the town garbage dump.... The stench was awful. The eyes I peered into seemed hollow and hopeless.... But the need, as dire as it was, was not nearly as impactful as the love I saw in one of the young orphaned boys." Moved by his encounter and firsthand glimpse of extreme poverty, Stewart felt led by God for him and his congregation to take responsibility for the "kind of church" they had been: one that ignored the cries of the global poor, that had propagated the idea of contemporary consumer Christianity, and that had produced consumers rather than disciples.

As a result of this journey, the church took out a full-page ad in the *Dallas Morning News* that read:

We Were Wrong
We followed trends
when we should have followed Jesus.
We told others how to live
but did not listen ourselves.
We live in the land of plenty,
denying ourselves nothing,
while ignoring our neighbors
who actually have nothing.
We sat on the sidelines doing nothing
while AIDS ravaged Africa.
We were wrong; we're sorry.
Please forgive us.

The ad included the church's name, phone number, and website. Stewart describes the decision: "This was no gimmick. We had nothing to gain from it but the disdain of the Christian community and the hope of restored credibility in the eyes of the unbelieving community."

The public response was overwhelming. Inundated with phone calls, the vast majority of which were affirming, the church had begun a journey of living out their changed behavior by more holistically engaging with communities around the world and communities in the United States. You can read more about this church's story in *We Were Wrong: An Evangelical Pastor's Confession and Stunning Realization of How Significant the Poor are in God's Redemptive Plans.*

This book has attempted to offer up lament in order to engage in the practice of corporate confession. Laments are found all over the Scriptures. The number of laments found in the book of Psalms is severely underrepresented in our hymns, worship songs, and in our corporate prayer life. Lament brings the focus back to God. We do not fix the world with our triumphalistic exceptionalism; instead, we recognize how deeply we need God to fix us. In our effort to fix the world's problems, we fail to engage our own culpability while focusing on the failures of others. The problem with the church is not the world out there, but the failures within. We cannot blame the world for their sinful actions and decisions when we do not confess our own. This text has been an attempt to reintroduce the discipline of confession and lament to the American church. It is a necessary part of our discipleship as a Christian community and our expression of our witness to the world.

Will you join us in this confession to the world?

"Forgive Us."

notes

Foreword

1. Ibrahim Abdul-Matin, *Green Deen: What Islam Teaches about Protecting the Planet*, from a book reading at Hue-Man Bookstore, November 12, 2010.

2. The New Revised Standard Version of Nehemiah 5:5 reads: "Now our flesh is the same as that of our kindred; our children are the same as their children; and yet we are forcing our sons and daughters to be slaves, and some of our daughters have been ravished; we are powerless, and our fields and vineyards now belong to others." The Contemporary English Version uses the word "rape" instead of "ravish." The actual Hebrew word, *kabash*, means "to conquer," "to violate," "to force," or "to bring into subjection." In the context of the actual text, it makes more sense that the writer meant what we now understand as rape. The phrase directly before it says "our sons and daughters are being forced into

slavery." It would be redundant to repeat that the daughters had been sold into slavery. The CEV version adds new information in the next phrase. For this reason, we believe the CEV version is the most accurate in this case.

3. See also Denise Hopkins, *Journey Through the Psalms* (Atlanta: Chalice Press, 2002), 5–6; and Glenn Pemberton, *Hurting with God* (Abilene, Tex.: Christian University Press, 2012). Both books point toward the absence of lament in Christian worship in the US.

4. The Hebrew word *geber* is alternatively translated as "everyman," "the valiant man," or simply "the man" or "the one." The *Brown-Driver-Briggs Lexicon* defines *geber* as "man as strong, distinguished from women, children, and non-combatants whom he is to defend." Francis Brown with S. R. Driver and Charles A. Briggs, *The New Brown-Driver–Briggs-Gesenius Hebrew and English Lexicon* (Peabody, Mass.: Hendrickson, 1974), 150. See also Kathleen M. O'Connor, *Lamentations and the Tears of the World* (Maryknoll, N.Y.: Orbis), 46–48.

5. Stephen Mott, *Biblical Ethics and Social Change* (New York: Oxford University Press, 1982), 4–21.

6. David Moberg, *The Great Reversal* (Eugene, Ore.: Wipf & Stock, 2007).

Chapter 1: Sins against God's Creation

1. Alan Taylor, "'Wasty Ways': Stories of American Settlement," in *American Environmental History,* ed. Louis S. Warren (Oxford: Blackwell, 2003), 111.

2. Ibid., 112.

3. Ibid., 113.

4. William Cronon, "The Trouble with Wilderness, or,

Getting Back to the Wrong Nature," *American Environmental History,* ed. Louis S. Warren (Oxford: Blackwell Publishing, 2003), 215.

5. Ibid., 115.

6. Ibid., 215.

7. Taylor, " 'Wasty Ways,' " 114.

8. Cronon, "The Trouble with Wilderness" 215.

9. Ibid., 217.

10. Ibid., 217.

11. Ibid., 224.

12. Lisa Sharon Harper and D. C. Innes, *Left, Right, and Christ: Evangelical Faith in Politics* (Boise: Russell Media, 2011), 201.

13. Ronald D. Eller, *Uneven Ground: Appalachia Since 1945* (Lexington, Ky.: The University Press of Kentucky, 2008), 91.

14. Ibid., 4.

15. Ibid., 102.

16. Ibid., 123.

17. Ibid., 6.

18. Ibid., 120.

19. W. Lee Daniels and Collaborators, "Properties and Reclamation of Coal Refuse Disposal Areas," *International Affiliation of Land Reclamationists,* www.landrehab.org (accessed January 25, 2014).

20. Eller, *Uneven Ground,* 163.

21. Ibid., 164.

22. Ibid., 167.

23. Harper and Innes, *Left, Right, and Christ,* 201.

24. Ibid.

25. CitzenLink Staff, "A Skeptics Guide to Debunking Global Warming Alarmism: Uncovering the Truth about Global Warming," *Citizen Link* (June 18, 2010): http://www.citizenlink.com/2010/06/18/a-skeptic%E2%80%99s-guide-to-debunking-global-warming-alarmism/ (accessed 25 January 2014).

26. Michael S. Northcott, *The Environment and Christian Ethics* (New York: Cambridge University Press, 1996), 39.

27. Ibid., 326.

28. "Outdoor Water Use in the United States," *United States Environmental Protection Agency*, http://www.epa.gov/WaterSense/pubs/outdoor.html (accessed July 11, 2013).

29. "Water for Life Decade: Human Right to Water," *United Nations*, http://www.un.org/waterforlifedecade/human_right_to_water.shtml (accessed July 11, 2013).

30. Northcott, *The Environment and Christian Ethics*, 325–26.

31. Jonathan Merritt, *Green Like God: Unlocking the Divine Plan for Our Planet* (New York: Faith Words, 2010), 2.

32. Ibid., 158.

33. Walter Brueggemann opens his book, *Peace* (St. Louis: Chalice Press, 2001), with a vision of humanity's relationship to creation that challenges the pervasive view that humanity was created to exist apart from creation. Brueggemann states: "The central vision of world history in the Bible is that all of creation is one, every creature in community with every other, living in harmony and security toward the joy and well-being of every other creature."

34. See Conrad Hyers, *The Meaning of Creation: Genesis and Modern Science* (Atlanta: John Knox Press, 1984).

35. Late sixteenth- and early seventeenth-century contemporaries Sir Francis Bacon, the father of the scientific method, and the French philosopher René Descartes are often credited by scholars with laying the foundations of the Western worldview of environmental ethics. In an article entitled "The Man-Nature Relationship and Environmental Ethics," published in the May 2003 edition of the Belgium-based *Journal of Environmental Radioactivity*, Ph. Bourdeau explained: "For Francis Bacon we must subdue nature, penetrate its secrets and chain it to satisfy our desires. Man is the center of the world and the object of science is to dominate nature. The same idea was taken up by Descartes who stated that we should use science to make us 'masters and possessors of nature.'"

36. See F. Forrester Church, *The Essential Tillich: An Anthology of the Writings of Paul Tillich,* (Chicago: University of Chicago Press, 1999), 195.

37. Steve Connor, science editor for *The Independent*, reported in a July 2010 article entitled, "Microscopic Life Crucial to the Marine Food Chain Is Dying Out: The Consequences Could Be Catastrophic," that a new scientific study reported that over the past century 40 percent of phytoplankton (the microscopic plants that provide much of the world's oxygen) in the world's oceans has died. Much of that loss has occurred since the 1950s: www.independent.co.uk/environment/climate-change/the-dead-sea-global-warming-blamed-for-40-per-cent-decline-in-the-oceans-phytoplankton-2038074.html.

38. "Deforestation and Greenhouse Gases," Congressional Budget Office Report, *Congressional*

Budget Office (January 6, 2012): http://www.cbo.gov/publication/42686.

39. See "Agriculture: Mono-Cropping," *Global Environmental Governance Project*: http://www.environmentalgover nance.org/research/issues/agriculture/.

40. See "*Times* Topics: Genetically Modified Food," *New York Times*: http://topics.nytimes.com/top/reference/timestopics/subjects/g/genetically_modified_food/index. html.

41. The Potsdam Institute for Climate Impact Research and Climate Analytics, "Turn Down the Heat: Climate Extremes, Regional Impacts, and the Case for Resilience," 3–4.

Chapter 2: Sins against Indigenous People

1. Alan Taylor, *American Colonies: The Settling of North America* (New York: Penguin, 2001), 10.

2. Ibid., 40.

3. Ibid., 45.

4. Ibid., 21.

5. Ibid., 43.

6. Andrea Smith, *Conquest: Sexual Violence and American Indian Genocide* (Cambridge, Mass.: South End Press, 2005), 52.

7. Douglas Sweeney, *The American Evangelical Story: A History of the Movement* (Grand Rapids, Mich.: Baker, 2005), 82.

8. Alan Taylor, *American Colonies*, 197.

9. Ibid., 78.

10. Ibid., 112.

11. Ibid., 135.

12. Robert N. Barger, "Puritans," lecture, prepared by Kay Kizer, *University of Notre Dame* website (June 15, 2004): http://www3.nd.edu/~rbarger/www7/puritans.html (accessed January 25, 2014).

13. Vine Deloria Jr., *God is Red* (New York: Delta, 1973), 251.

14. Smith, *Conquest*, 36.

15. Ibid., 37.

16. Ibid., 41.

17. James Roark, Michael Johnson, Patricia Cline Cohen, Sarah Stage, Alan Lawson and Susan Hartmann, *The American Promise: A Compact History.* 4th ed. (Boston: Bedford and St. Martin's Press, 2010), 416. The five nations were the Cherokee, the Chickasaw, the Choctaw, the Creek, and the Seminole nations. They were considered "civilized" because they had already adopted many of the colonists' customs and had acculturated to British and European customs more than other indigenous groups.

18. John Ehle, *Trail of Tears: The Rise and Fall of the Cherokee Nation* (New York: Anchor Books, 1988), 94.

19. Ibid., 35.

20. Ibid., 222.

21. Ibid., 225.

22. Ibid., 59.

23. Deloria Jr., *God is Red*, 249.

24. Ehle, *Trail of Tears*, 264.

25. Deloria Jr., *God is Red*, 24.

26. Ibid., 205.

27. Dee Brown, *Bury My Heart at Wounded Knee* (New York: Macmillan, 2001), 86–87.

28. "National Affairs: Soldier's Burial," *Time* (September 10, 1951): www.time.com/time/magazine/article/0,9171,815314,00.html.

29. Deloria Jr., *God is Red*, 185.

30. Ibid., 185.

31. Ibid., 23.

32. Mae Cannon, *Social Justice Handbook: Small Steps for a Better World* (Downers Grove, Ill.: InterVarsity, 2009), 48.

33. The Gene Autry Museum of the West Exhibit (circa 2004), featured *American Progress* and demonstrated the ways the image of Columbia had been used on brochures and in advertisements to lure people to the West since that time.

34. See Richard Twiss, *One Church Many Tribes: Following Jesus the Way God Made You* (Ventura, Calif.: Regal, 2000).

35. Representing a conservative perspective, David Innes, coauthor of *Left, Right, and Christ: Evangelical Faith in Politics*, reflects in his chapter on environmentalism that "while Christian environmentalists agree that we are stewards of the earth for God's sake, they often miss or underappreciate this definitive feature of Christian stewardship.... As we read in the parable of the talents, it's more like the stewardship of an investment banker or trust fund manager, one who takes something of value and develops it into something of much greater value." Innes continues, quipping: "Today Manhattan Island

is a radical improvement over what it was when Peter Minuit bought it from the Lenape Indians for the industrious Dutch. Now it's a center of world transforming creativity, enterprise, and wealth production."

36. John Winthrop, "City Upon a Hill," *Mount Holyoke*, sermon (1630): https://www.mtholyoke.edu/acad/intrel/winthrop.htm.

37. Ibid.

38. Ibid.

39. By wealth, we do not mean an overflow of rubies, pearls, and gold coins. Rather, we mean the accumulation of assets upon which society bases its stability; assets that can be sold for profit. The Puritans' greatest asset pursuit was that of land. In Western civilization land has always been the most valuable asset. It has triggered wars between nations and intrigues between households and has even the underlying reasons for matrimonial unions. In the Western world land is wealth.

40. It is worth noting that wealth is not inherently evil. Money is just money. It is worth the value people assign to it. The idolatry of money is what is evil. Idols set themselves up in direct opposition to God. Idols demand allegiance. Jesus warned his disciples about the way money, by its nature, will demand allegiance. It will call good people to hate God in order to love money. For money does not only demand allegiance, but its ways are counter to the ways of Christ. Money will demand that it becomes the highest priority of the one who bows to it—a higher priority than the protection of people made in the image of God. Our response to money's demand is where the evil or the good resides.

41. Francis Bremer, *John Winthrop: America's Forgotten Founding Father* (New York: Oxford University Press, 2003), 267.

Chapter 3: Sins against African Americans and People of Color

1. Albert Raboteau, *Slave Religion: The "Invisible Institution" in the Antebellum South* (Oxford: Oxford University Press, 2004), 96.

2. Ibid., 100–101.

3. Albert Raboteau, *A Fire in the Bones: Reflections on African-American Religious History* (Boston: Beacon Press, 1995), 18.

4. Edmund S. Morgan, *American Slavery, American Freedom* (New York: Norton, 1975), Kindle Locations 6892–6895.

5. Raboteau, *A Fire in the Bones*, 19.

6. Albert Raboteau, *Canaan Land: A Religious History of African Americans* (Oxford: Oxford University Press, 2001), Kindle Location 94.

7. Christine Heyrman, *Southern Cross: The Beginnings of the Bible Belt* (New York: Knopf, 1997), Kindle Locations 4936–4939.

8. Stephen R. Haynes, *Noah's Curse: The Biblical Justification of American Slavery* (Oxford: Oxford University Press, 2002), Kindle Locations 1066–1068.

9. Ibid., Kindle Locations 1356–1358.

10. Ibid., Kindle Locations 1566–1569.

11. Ibid., Kindle Locations 1982–1983.

12. Ibid., Kindle Locations 2029–2030.

13. Ibid., Kindle Locations 2304–2306.

14. Ibid., Kindle Locations 2037–2039.

15. James Cone, *The Cross and the Lynching Tree* (New York: Orbis, 2011), 30–31.

16. Ibid., 39.

17. Ibid., 49.

18. Troy Jackson, *Becoming King: Martin Luther King Jr. and the Making of a National Leader* (Lexington: University Press of Kentucky, 2008), 13–14.

19. Ibid., 25.

20. Ibid., 165.

21. Ibid., 121.

22. Ibid., 118.

23. Haynes, *Noah's Curse*, Kindle locations 1313–1319.

24. Michael Emerson and Christian Smith, *Divided by Faith: Evangelical Religion and the Problem of Race in America* (Oxford: Oxford University Press, 2000).

25. Michelle Alexander, *The New Jim Crow: Mass Incarceration in the Age of Colorblindness* (New York: The New Press, 2010), Kindle locations 304–20.

26. Drew Magary, "What the Duck?" *Gentleman's Quarterly* (January 2014): http://www.gq.com/entertainment/television/201401/duck-dynasty-phil-robertson.

27. G. C. Berkouwer, *Sin* (Grand Rapids, Mich.: Eerdmans, 1971), 281.

28. John Stott, *The Cross of Christ* (Downers Grove, Ill.: InterVarsity, 1990), 188.

29. See chapter 6: "Sins against Immigrants" for a discussion on supersessionism and its impact on elevating whiteness above all other categories.

30. Louis Menand, *The Metaphysical Club* (New York: Farrar, Straus & Giroux, 2002), 104–5.

31. Ibid., 105.

32. Willie James Jennings, *The Christian Imagination* (New Haven, Conn.: Yale University Press, 2010), 58–59.

33. John Willinsky, *Learning to Divide the World* (Minneapolis: University of Minnesota Press, 2000), 208.

34. Ibid., 193, 197.

35. Virginia Dominguez, "Invoking Culture: The Messy Side of Cultural Politics," in *Eloquent Obsessions*, ed. Marianna Torgovnick (Durham, N.C.: Duke University Press, 1994), 254.

36. Ibid., 247–48.

37. Jennings, *Christian Imagination*, 35.

38. Ibid., 40–64.

39. Ibid., 21.

40. Ibid., 58.

Chapter 4: Sins against Women

1. "Robertson's Letter Attacks Feminists," *New York Times* (August 26. 1992): www.nytimes.com/1992/08/26/us/robertson-letter-attacks-feminists.html (accessed January 26, 2014).

2. John Demos, *Entertaining Satan: Witchcraft and the Culture of Early New England* (Oxford: Oxford University Press, 1982), 10–12.

3. Frances Hill, *A Delusion of Satan: The Full Story of the Salem Witch Trials* (Cambridge, Mass.: De Capo, 1995), 22.

4. See Hill, *A Delusion of Satan*, 31. See also Carol F.

Karlsen, *The Devil in the Shape of a Woman: Witchcraft in Colonial New England* (New York: Norton, 1987), 47–50.

5. Karlsen, *Devil in the Shape of a Woman*, 119.

6. Ibid., 47–51.

7. Nell Irvin Painter, *Sojourner Truth: A Life, A Symbol* (New York: Norton, 1996), 14–17.

8. Ibid., 121–31. See also pages 164–78 where Painter reveals that the contemporary stories of Truth's Akron speech do not mention a hostile crowd or the repeated use of the phrase "Ar'n't I a woman?" Abolitionist and feminist Frances Dana Gage penned this apocryphal rendering of the event over a decade later.

9. Mae Cannon, *Social Justice Handbook* (Downers Grove, Ill.: InterVarsity, 2009), 58.

10. Painter, *Sojourner Truth*, 138–39.

11. Steven Buechler, *Women's Movements in the United States: Woman Suffrage, Equal Rights, and Beyond* (New Brunswick, N.J.: Rutgers University Press, 1990), 180.

12. Kathi Kern, *Mrs. Stanton's Bible* (Ithaca, N.Y.: Cornell University Press, 2001), 19.

13. Ibid., 48.

14. W. J. Conybeare and J. S. Howson, *The Life and Epistles of St. Paul, Vol. 1* (New York: Scribner, 1890), 60. See also Kern, *Mrs. Stanton's Bible*, 244–45, fn. 129.

15. Kern, *Mrs. Stanton's Bible*, 86.

16. Ibid., 97.

17. Ibid., 135.

18. Ibid., 4–5.

19. Ibid., 5.

20. Donald T. Critchlow, *Phyllis Schlafly and Grassroots Conservatism* (Princeton: Princeton University Press, 2005), 215.

21. Ibid., 216.

22. Ibid., 218.

23. Ibid., 221.

24. Buechler, *Women's Movements in the United States*, 189 – 90.

25. "Domestic Violence: Abuse Statistics," Statistic Brain Research Institute: http://www.statisticbrain.com/domestic-violence-abuse-stats/.

26. Women's Ministries Justice for Women Working Group, National Council of Churches USA: http://www.ncccusa.org/womensministry/domesticviolence2.html.

27. Jeff Crippen and Anna Wood, *A Cry for Justice: How the Evil of Domestic Abuse Hides in Your Church* (Amityville, N.Y.: Calvary Press, 2012), Kindle Locations 51 – 53.

28. Ibid., Kindle Locations 192 – 201.

29. John Sailhamer notes that "the one God created man through an expression of his plurality. Following this clue the divine plurality expressed in v.26 is seen as an anticipation of human plurality of the man and woman, thus casting the human relationship between man and woman in the role of reflecting God's own personal relationship with himself." John H. Sailhamer, "Genesis," in *The Expositor's Bible Commentary, Vol. 2*, ed. Frank E. Gaebelein (Grand Rapids, Mich.: Zondervan, 1990), 38.

30. Gleason L. Archer Jr., R. Laird Harris, and Bruce K. Waltke, *Theological Wordbook of the Old Testament, Vol. II* (Chicago: Moody, 1980), 660 – 61.

31. Craig Keener notes that "Jewish piety warned men not

to talk much with women.... Judaism did not have much regard for the witness of a woman, and the witness of an adulteress would be worthless." Craig S. Keener, *The Bible Background Commentary: New Testament* (Downers Grove, Ill: InterVarsity, 1993), 274.

32. Ibid., 551.

33. Ibid., 551. See also Andrew Lincoln, "Ephesians," in *Word Biblical Commentary* (Dallas: Word, 1990), 366.

34. John Kohlenberger III, "From Male Superiority to Mutual Submission," *Christian Management Report* (March/April 2000), 15 – 16, www.cbeinternational.org.

Chapter 5: Sins against the LGBTQ Community

1. David Johnson, *The Lavender Scare: The Cold War Persecution of Gays and Lesbians in the Federal Government* (Chicago: University of Chicago Press, 2004), 2.

2. Ibid., 38.

3. Eric Marcus, *Making Gay History: The Half-Century Fight for Lesbian and Gay Equal Rights* (New York: Perennial, 2002), 121 – 22.

4. Michael Bronski, *A Queer History of the United States* (Boston: Beacon Press, 2011), 219 – 20.

5. Anita Bryant, *The Anita Bryant Story: The Survival of Our Nation's Families and the Threat of Militant Homosexuality* (Old Tappan, N.J.: Revell, 1977), 38.

6. Ibid., 55 – 56.

7. Bronski, *A Queer History of the United States*, 221.

8. Bryant, *The Anita Bryant Story*, 62.

9. Ibid., 114.

10. Arlene Stein, *The Stranger Next Door: The Story of a Small Community's Battle Over Sex, Faith, and Civil Rights* (Boston: Beacon Press, 2001), 28–29.

11. James Dobson, "Your Family Resource," *Dr. James Dobson's Family Talk* (2012): http://drjamesdobson.org/about/commentaries/your-family-resource.

12. Bronski, *A Queer History of the United States*, 226.

13. Jack Nichols, *The Gay Agenda: Talking Back to the Fundamentalists* (Amherst, N.Y.: Prometheus, 1996), 140.

14. Ibid., 56.

15. Marcus, *Making Gay History*, 449–50.

16. John Stott, *Romans* (Downers Grove, Ill.: InterVarsity, 1994), 109.

17. George Marsden, *Fundamentalism and American Culture* (New York: Oxford University Press, 2006), 15.

18. Robert Putnam and David Campbell, *American Grace* (New York: Simon & Schuster, 2010), 80–120.

19. C. S. Lewis, *Mere Christianity* (New York: Collier, 1943), 111.

20. Jer Swigart, interview by Mae Elise Cannon, October 4, 2013, in Washington, D.C.

21. Ibid.

Chapter 6: Sins against Immigrants

1. Emma Lazarus and Josephine Lazarus, *The Poems of Emma Lazarus, Vol. 1* (New York: Houghton Mifflin, 1889), 203.

2. Ray Allen Billington, *The Protestant Crusade 1800–1860: A Study of the Origins of American Nativism* (Chicago: Quadrangle, 1964), 1–5.

3. Ibid., 42–43.

4. Debby Applegate, *The Most Famous Man in America: The Biography of Henry Ward Beecher* (New York: Doubleday, 2006), 86, 111.

5. Billington, *The Protestant Crusade 1800-1860,* 70–74.

6. Ibid., 76.

7. Ibid., 86.

8. Peter Schrag, *Not Fit for Our Society: Immigration and Nativism in America* (Berkeley: University of California Press, 2010), 19–20.

9. Billington, *The Protestant Crusade 1800–1860,* 194–95.

10. Ibid., 199–200.

11. Schrag, *Not Fit for Our Society,* 28.

12. Dale T. Knobel, *"America for the Americans": The Nativist Movement in the United States* (New York: Twayne, 1996), 82–83.

13. Billington, *The Protestant Crusade 1800–1860,* 325.

14. Schrag, *Not Fit for Our Society,* 29–34.

15. Ibid., 34.

16. Matthew Frye Jacobson, *Whiteness of a Different Color: European Immigrants and the Alchemy of Race* (Cambridge: Harvard University Press, 1998), 73.

17. Jerome R. Adams, *Gringos and Greasers: The Historical Roots of Anglo-Hispanic Prejudice* (Jefferson, N.C.: McFarland, 2006), 167.

18. Joe R. Feagin, "Old Poison in New Bottles," in *Immigrants Out!* ed. Juan F. Perea (New York: NYU Press, 1996), 15.

19. Ibid., 20.

20. John Higham, *Strangers in the Land: Patterns of*

American Nativism, 1860–1925 (New Brunswick, N.J.: Rutgers University Press, 1983), 38.

21. Knobel, *"America for the Americans,"* 195–96.

22. Schrag, *Not Fit for Our Society,* 49.

23. Higham, *Strangers in the Land,* 40.

24. Knobel, *"America for the Americans,"* 196.

25. Gary Dorrien, *Soul in Society: The Making and Renewal of Social Christianity* (Minneapolis: Fortress, 1995), 43.

26. Knobel, *"America for the Americans,"* 210.

27. Robert F. Martin, *Hero of the Heartland: Billy Sunday and the Transformation of American Society, 1862–1935* (Bloomington: Indiana University Press, 2002), 134–35.

28. Knobel, *"America for the Americans,"* 262–63.

29. Ibid., 270.

30. Ibid., 198.

31. John Higham, *Strangers in the Land,* 302.

32. Knobel, *"America for the Americans,"* 260.

33. Ibid., see also Peter Schrag, *Not Fit for Our Society,* 120–22.

34. Schrag, *Not Fit for Our Society,* 126.

35. Ibid., 130.

36. Ibid., 127–29.

37. Ibid., 103.

38. Ibid., 153.

39. Ibid., 160–61.

40. Ibid., 166.

41. Ibid., 212.

42. Jerry Falwell, "The Candidate Who Can Win in 2008," in *WND Commentary* (August 26, 2006): www.wnd.com/ 2006/08/37628/ (accessed February 3, 2014).

43. Evangelicals for Biblical Immigration Facebook Page: www.facebook.com/pages/Evangelicals-for-Biblical-Immigration-EBI/208457102639014.

44. Steve King, speech at anti-immigration Virginia rally, quoted in Seung Min Kim, "Steve King Hits the Road on Immigration," *Politico* (August 12, 2013): www.politico .com/story/2013/08/steve-king-hits-the-road-on-immigra tion-95458.html#ixzz2c3Z4jEQ5.

45. Steve King, "Rep. Steve King Slams Norquist over Attacks on Immigration," interview by Todd Beaman and John Bachman, *Newsmax* (July 18, 2013): www.newsmax.com/ Newsfront/king-norquist-attacks-immigration/2013/07/18/ id/515882.

46. Jennings, *The Christian Imagination*, 6.

47. Walter Brueggemann, *The Prophetic Imagination* (Minneapolis: Fortress, 2001), 3.

48. William Cavanaugh, *Torture and Eucharist* (Malden, Mass.: Blackwell, 1998), 57.

49. Jennings, *The Christian Imagination*, 6.

50. Charles Hodge, *Systematic Theology Vol. II* (New York: Scribner, 1965), 99.

51. Thomas Maston, *The Bible and Race* (Nashville: Broadman, 1959), 12.

52. Matthew Frye Jacobson, *Barbarian Virtues* (New York: Hill and Wang, 2001), 83 Emphasis added.

53. Ibid., 126.

54. On page 17 of *Barbarian Virtues*, Jacobson alludes to the

connection between missionary effort and the expansion of commerce. Jacobson cites Josiah Strong's statement that "The world is to be Christianized and civilized.... What is the process of civilizing but *the creating of more and higher wants? ...* The millions of Africa and Asia are someday to have the wants of a Christian civilization" (emphasis added). Jacobson argues that "commerce would follow the missionary." Jacobson sees the Christian perspective in America as being both the "spiritual savior and industrial supplier." The Christian imagination sought to replicate the consumerism of American society throughout the world.

55. Emil Brunner, *Man in Revolt* (Philadelphia: Westminster, 1939), 140.

56. Jennings, *The Christian Imagination*, 8.

57. In *The Christian Imagination*, Jennings asserts that "it is a truism to say that humans are all bound to the earth. However, that articulated connection to the earth comes under profound and devastating alteration with the age of discovery and colonialism" (40). "It was a theological form — an inverted, distorted vision of creation that reduced theological anthropology to commodified bodies. In this inversion, whiteness replaced the earth as the signifier of identities" (58). "With the emergence of whiteness, identity was calibrated through possession of, not possession by specific land" (59).

58. Stuart Banner, *How the Indians Lost Their Land: Law and Power on the Frontier* (Cambridge, Mass.: Harvard University Press, 2005), 33.

59. Ibid., 12.

60. See Michael Wyschogrod, *Abraham's Promise: Judaism and Jewish-Christian Relations* (Grand Rapids, Mich.:

Eerdmans, 2004). Wyschogrod makes the argument that a high level of insecurity is related to this diseased imagination. On page 200 of his essay "Paul, Jews, and Gentiles," he asserts: "Judaism has rarely understood the depth of the Gentiles' feeling of exclusion. Because Jews have experienced persecution and rejection for so long, it has been difficult for them to understand that there are Gentiles, and not a few, who wish to become members of the family that is the Jewish people."

61. David Novack, "From Supersessionism to Parallelism in Jewish-Christian Dialogue," in *Talking with Christians: Musings of a Jewish Theologian* (Grand Rapids, Mich.: Eerdmans, 2005), 12.

62. Thomas Torrance notes that "the covenant between God and Israel was not a covenant between God and a holy people, but precisely the reverse. It was a covenant established out of pure grace between God and Israel in its sinful, rebellious and estranged existence. Hence, no matter how rebellious or sinful Israel was, it could not escape from the covenant love and faithfulness of God." Thomas F. Torrance, *The Mediation of Christ* (Colorado Springs: Helmers & Howard, 1992), 27.

63. J. Kameron Carter, *Race: A Theological Account* (New York: Oxford University Press, 2008), 35.

64. Ibid., 229.

65. Ibid., 6.

66. Ibid., 5.

Chapter 7: Sins against Jews and Muslims

1. Fuad Sha'ban, *For Zion's Sake: The Judeo-Christian Tradition in American Culture* (Ann Harbor, Mich.: Pluto Press, 2005), 12.

2. Adam Taylor, *Mobilizing Hope: Faith-Inspired Activism for a Post-Civil Rights Generation* (Downers Grove, Ill.: InterVarsity, 2010), Kindle Editions 180–181.

3. Peggy Noonan, "On American Exceptionalism," *Wall Street Journal* (September 13, 2013): http://online.wsj.com/article/D0E047A9-6752-45F2-AD32-2C1A3A88DC00.html#!D0E047A9-6752-45F2-AD32-2C1A3A88DC00 (accessed January 25, 2014).

4. Fuad Sha'ban, *For Zion's Sake*, 12.

5. Charles Marsh, *The Beloved Community: How Faith Shapes Social Justice, from the Civil Rights Movement to Today* (New York: Basic Books, 2005), 7.

6. Taylor, *Mobilizing Hope*, Kindle Editions 180.

7. Richard Land, *The Divided States of America* (Nashville: Nelson, 2007), 37.

8. Alan Dershowitz, *The Case for Israel* (Hoboken, N.J.: Wiley, 2003), 2.

9. Claudia Koonz notes that "with little encouragement from party or state, Protestant leaders sponsored the Institute for the Study and Eradication of Jewish Influence in German Religious Life. Given Hitler's and Himmler's contempt for organized Christianity, it is not surprising that antisemitic theologians received relatively little recognition despite their efforts. The scholarly initiative to purge the 'Jewish spirit' from the Christian *Volk* offered a chance for Protestant theologians to

demonstrate their usefulness to a regime that spurned their collaboration. One of their major projects demonstrated that Jesus had been born to Armenian, not Jewish, parents." Claudia Koonz, *The Nazi Conscience* (Cambridge, Mass.: Harvard University Press, 2003), 212–13.

10. Richard Land, *The Divided States of America*, 45.

11. Ussama Makdisi, *Faith Misplaced: The Broken Promise of U.S.–Arab Relations: 1820–2001* (New York: Perseus, 2010), 20.

12. Mae Elise Cannon, "Mischief Making in Palestine: American Protestant Christian Attitudes toward the Holy Land, 1917–1949," *Cultural Encounters* 7, no. 1 (2011): 57.

13. William H. Swatos, "Glock, Charles Young," *Encyclopedia of Religion and Society*: http://hirr.hartsem.edu/ency/glock.htm (accessed September 30, 2013).

14. Charles Glock, "Churchly Particularism and the Jews: A Trifaith Symposium on the Glock-Stark Anti-Semitism Survey," *The Christian Century* (August 10, 1966), 987.

15. Alan Dershowitz, *The Case for Israel*, 211.

16. Tony Maalouf, *Arabs in the Shadow of Israel: The Unfolding of God's Prophetic Plan for Ishmael's Line* (Grand Rapids, Mich.: Kregel, 2003), 32.

17. Fuad Sha'ban. *For Zion's Sake*, 11.

18. Ibid., 13.

19. Ibid., 17.

20. Ibid., xv.

21. Ibid.

22. Ibid.

23. Ibid.

24. Ibid., xvi–xvii.

25. Damien Cave, "Far from Ground Zero, Obscure Pastor is Ignored No Longer," *The New York Times* (August 25, 2010): www.nytimes.com/2010/08/26/us/26gainesville .html?_r=0.

26. Ibid.

27. Enayat Najafizada and Rod Nordland, "Afghans Avenge Florida Koran Burning, Killing 12," *New York Times* (April 1, 2011): www.nytimes.com/2011/04/02/world/ asia/02afghanistan.html?pagewanted=all.

28. Taunya Lovell Banks, "Dangerous Woman: Elizabeth Key's Freedom Suit—Subjecthood and Racialized Identity in Seventeenth Century Colonial Virginia," *Akron Law Review* 41 (2008): 799–827.

29. Ibid., 825, fn. 141.

30. Ibid., 827.

31. Robert Seitz Frey, "Christian Responses to the Trial and Lynching of Leo Frank: Ministers, Theologians, and Laymen," *The Georgia Historical Quarterly* 71, no. 3 (Fall, 1987): 461–64.

32. Ibid., 465.

33. Ibid.

34. James H. Cone, *The Cross and the Lynching Tree* (Maryknoll, N.Y.: Orbis, 2011), 7.

35. See Philip Schaff, *America: A Sketch of the Political, Social, and Religious Character of the United States of North America* (New York: Scribner, 1855), 55.

36. Ibid.

37. David Gruben, "The Jewish Americans," *PBS* (2007):

www.pbs.org/jewishamericans/jewish_life/anti-semitism.
html.

38. Michael Dobbs, "Ford and GM Scrutinized for Alleged
Nazi Collaboration," *Washington Post* (November 30,
1998): www.washingtonpost.com/wp-srv/national/daily/
nov98/nazicars30.htm.

39. Miroslav Volf, *A Public Faith: How Followers of Christ
Should Serve the Common Good* (Grand Rapids, Mich.:
Brazos, 2011), 40.

40. Ibid.

41. Omar Sacirbey, "Anti-Sharia Bill Passed in North
Carolina Without Governor Pat McCrory's Signature,"
Huffington Post (August 27, 2013): http://www.huffing
tonpost.com/2013/08/27/anti-sharia-bill-north-carolina-
gov-pat-mccrory_n_3823796.html.

acknowledgments

Mae Elise Cannon

This project has been a deeply transformative experience. I am grateful to Troy Jackson for reaching out to me about this project several years ago. Over the years, as the project progressed, it was a great privilege to join in partnership and friendship with both Soong-Chan Rah and Lisa Sharon Harper. I hope the relationship we possess as authors is a small glimpse of the King's beloved community.

Many amazing people contributed to the thoughts and ideas shared in this book, including Randy Woodley, Andrea Smith, Paul Louis Metzger, Peter Heltzel, Sandra Van Opstal, Mimi Haddad, and many others who are a part of our extended Evangelicals for Justice (E4J) community. I am grateful for the wealth and diversity of thought and experience that constitutes a movement of evangelicals committed to the gospel of Christ and its full fruition of both righteousness and justice. I also am indebted to family and loved ones for their support and love along the way.

Lisa Sharon Harper

I am deeply indebted to the Intervarsity Christian Fellowship community who grounded me with such a deep love for and trust of Scripture. Our work together toward ethnic reconciliation offered a profound experience in confronting the spiritual lies at work among us and introduced me to biblical scholar Dr. Terry McGonigal. I owe him a profound debt of appreciation. His work on the biblical concept of *shalom* has inspired and grounded my work for the past eleven years. I also owe a deep debt of gratitude to the Evangelicals for Justice, the Voices Project, and New York Faith and Justice communities, as well as my current co-laborers at Sojourners. You all continue to teach me what it looks like to not only say "Forgive me," but to do it. You are living witnesses of the gospel's power to transform the world.

Troy Jackson

This book began as a sermon series at University Christian Church in Cincinnati, where I served for nearly nineteen years. My work on this book is indeed inspired by University Christian Church and Rohs Street Cafe and by all my new friends in community organizing, including the Ohio Organizing Collaborative, PICO national network, the AMOS Project, ISAIAH, and Lifelines to Healing. Thank You!

Soong-Chan Rah

I offer my deepest gratitude to my academic mentors who have shaped my theological reflection on these particular issues. Willie Jennings, J. Kameron Carter, Eldin Villafane, Emmanuel Katongole, Kate Bowler, Amy Laura Hall, Grant Wacker, Sam Wells, Ellen Davis were all part of the community of scholars who have shaped my formation on these topics. As always, my wife, Sue, and my children, Annah and Elijah, served as my most treasured support during the writing process.